NELSON MANDELA

NELSON MANDELA

THE EARLY LIFE OF
ROLIHLAHLA MADIBA

JEAN GUILOINEAU

translated from the French by
Joseph Rowe

NORTH ATLANTIC BOOKS
BERKELEY, CALIFORNIA

Published by
North Atlantic Books
P.O. Box 12327
Berkeley, California 94712

Translated from *Nelson Mandela: Naissance d'un destin,* Éditions Autrement, 1998

Printed in the United States of America
Cover and book design © Ayelet Maida, A/M Studios
Cover photo courtesy of UWC: Robben Island Musum Mayibuye Archives
Interior photos: Rights reserved; IDAF:SIPA, Jean Guiloineau, and Darryl Evans

Nelson Mandela: The Early Life of Rolihlahla Madiba is sponsored by the Society for the Study of Native Arts and Sciences, a nonprofit educational corporation whose goals are to develop an educational and crosscultural perspective linking various scientific, social, and artistic fields; to nurture a holistic view of arts, sciences, humanities, and healing; and to publish and distribute literature on the relationship of mind, body, and nature.

North Atlantic Books' publications are available through most bookstores. For further information, call 800-337-2665 or visit our website at www.northatlanticbooks.com.

Substantial discounts on bulk quantities are available to corporations, professional associations, and other organizations. For details and discount information, contact our special sales department.

Library of Congress Cataloging-in-Publication Data
Guiloineau, Jean, 1939–
    [Nelson Mandela, naissance d'un destin. English]
    Nelson Mandela : the early life of Rolihlahla Madiba / by Jean Guiloineau ; translated by Joseph Rowe.
        p. cm.
    ISBN 1-55643-417-0 (pbk.)
    1. Mandela, Nelson, 1918—Childhood and youth. 2. Presidents—South Africa—Biography. I. Title.
    DT1974 .G8513 2002
    968.06'5'092–dc21

                                                        2002011409

1 2 3 4 5 6 7 8 9 / 06 05 04 03 02

For Adèle,
who shook hands
with Rolihlahla

Contents

Even as a boy, I defeated my opponents without dishonoring them.

The first thing is to be honest with yourself. You can never have an impact on society if you have not changed yourself.

As we are liberated from our own fear, our presence automatically liberates others.

—Nelson Mandela

The Man Without a Face

The man who walked out of Victor Vester prison on February 11, 1990, had no face. Neither the hundreds of people waiting for him along Paarl Road, nor the thousands of others who would soon be cheering him from the city hall and balconies of Cape Town, nor the countless millions in front of TV screens all over the world would recognize the facial features of this living legend.

This man without a face, Nelson Rolihlahla Madiba Mandela, had been arrested on Sunday, August 5, 1962, in the Natal province, sixty miles north of Durban. He had been sentenced to five years in prison for speaking out in public, and for leaving South Africa illegally earlier that year. While serving this sentence, he was tried again for more serious charges connected with his leadership of the armed resistance group, Umkhonto we Sizwe. He and his colleagues were convicted of terrorism, narrowly escaping execution, receiving life sentences instead. He was forty-four years old at the time. He would be seventy-one when he was finally released from prison in 1990.

From the very beginning of Mandela's incarceration, the political authorities had forbidden anyone to take his photograph. Because of this ban, no one in all those years other than prison inmates, guards, and his family had seen the changing face of the man who had become the most famous—and the longest-detained—political prisoner in the world. The only exception to this was in

1966, in the early years of his long imprisonment. A photographer from the *London Daily Telegraph* was somehow able to take several pictures of Nelson Mandela inside the prison at Robben Island (also known as Seal Island), off the Atlantic coast, facing the Cape of Good Hope. On this occasion the prisoners had been given needles, thread, and old clothes to mend instead of the usual sledgehammers and picks they used for breaking up large rocks to be ground into gravel. Mandela would only consent to being photographed in the presence of his old friend and veteran of the struggle, Walter Sisulu. One of these photos shows the two men in conversation. Mandela is speaking with lowered eyes, the index finger of his right hand extended. In his left hand he is holding the thread with which he had been sewing. Behind Mandela and Sisulu, one can make out the prison yard. The clothes to be mended are lying upon stone slabs placed upon the ground. In another photo, Nelson Mandela is sitting on one of these slabs, mending what seems to be a very old shirt. He is forty-eight years old, and this is the last picture of him the world would see until 1990.

There were two reasons for this ban on photographs. The minor reason had its roots in an incident which he relates in his autobiography. One morning shortly after the prisoners' arrival at Robben Island, they were led into administration offices. First, their fingerprints were taken; then they were told to stand in line so they could be photographed individually. True to his role as lawyer and dissident, Mandela demanded to be shown the law which permitted the prison authorities to photograph them without their consent. Since no such law could be found, the photos were not taken.

Mandela explains that he refused to be photographed in prison clothes because he found it degrading. Thus the *London Daily Telegraph* photos of 1966 were a unique exception. But if we look carefully at the second of these, we see that he is not wearing pants, but long shorts that go almost to the knees. This is not visible in the frame of the other photo. The day of his arrival at Robben Island, Mandela stubbornly refused to wear these regulation shorts, which he judged to be a form of deliberate humiliation. After two weeks of protests, a guard tossed an old pair of trousers onto the floor of his cell. But then Mandela demanded that all other prisoners be given trousers as well. Finally, the prison warden himself intervened, telling him he could wear shorts or go naked.

This anecdote is a good example of the spirit of resistance and struggle which animated Nelson Mandela for most of his life. "Any person or institution which tries to rob me of my dignity has lost in advance, for this is something which I will never betray, for any reason," he has written. Perhaps it was this dignity which inspired him to compose a wry caption for the photograph of him in shorts: "Mending clothes at Pretoria prison before being sent to Robben Island." In order to appreciate this irony, one needs to know that prisoners wore trousers at Pretoria. Of course he knew the *London Daily Telegraph* photo was taken at Robben Island.

But the most important reason for the ban was the determination of the political authorities to make this prisoner (as troublesome inside as he had been outside) as invisible as possible. Unable to do away with him physically because of international pressure,[1] they decided to use his protest to their advantage and ban his photographic image. A special governmental decree was issued, which not only forbade photographs of the prisoner at Robben Island, but also prohibited any photograph of him to be published in South Africa.

Thus all public images of Nelson Mandela disappeared in South Africa, while in the outside world, only long-outdated photographs were available. Books about him often had to resort to an old photo of his marriage to Winnie in 1958, where he appears only

---

[1] However, the pressure was still largely weak and hypocritical at that time. On June 8, 1964, a few days before the sentencing of Mandela and his Rivonia colleagues, United Nations delegates from Morocco and Ivory Coast introduced a resolution demanding that South Africa refrain from executing these political prisoners. Three members of the Security Council abstained in this vote: The United States, Great Britain, and France.

as a silhouette—like a dark specter come to haunt the corridors of South African power.

The irony is that this strategy totally backfired. The more the authorities sought to rid the South African conscience of this accusing, threatening presence by depriving the people of his image, the more Mandela's mythic stature grew in response. It became immense, and his name became synonymous with the cry of freedom. By the time "Free Nelson Mandela!" had become a slogan which also meant "Free South Africa!" his political influence was already an irreversible and decisive factor.

About his underground period after 1960, Mandela wrote, "Becoming invisible is the key to clandestine operation. I became a creature of the night." Winnie later wrote of these days, "Life with him was also life without him." During this time newspapers referred to this elusive, invisible man as "the Black Pimpernel."[2]

Who would have dreamed that a day would come when those who had most wanted him to disappear would ultimately be the ones to seek him out in the depths of his prison—relieved that he had not really disappeared—so that he could help move the country away from the brink of catastrophe to which their policies had led it? Who could have imagined that it would be their images that would fade before his in the light of history?

There are times when absence can be more powerful than presence. During the long years that Mandela spent in prison, the situation in South Africa continued to deteriorate. It reached a peak of violence in 1976, when the children of Soweto, the huge southwestern ghetto of Johannesburg, rebelled against a law which required students to learn Afrikaans in school. This was the language of the Afrikaner ethnicity, the architects and promoters of apartheid. The repressive response of the authorities was extreme,

---

[2] A reference to the term "Scarlet Pimpernel," the hero of a series of novels by the English Baroness Emmuska Orczy.

provoking riots in black ghettos all over the country. The language issue was the spark that inflamed an already explosive situation.

Some of these children had not even been born when Mandela entered prison. What they were really rebelling against was the despair, the lifelessness, the absence of any believable future, in a system whose injustice had become intolerable. The official figures claim there were 618 dead and 1,500 wounded. The vast majority of these victims were less than seventeen years old. The first casualty was a child killed by a policeman's bullet. His name was Hector Peterson, and he was thirteen years old. In the following weeks, 13,553 people were sentenced to prison terms. Over 5,000 of them were under eighteen. Thousands of other youths fled the country to escape the repression. Many joined the army that the African National Congress (ANC) was trying to mount in Mozambique and Zimbabwe with the aim of liberating South Africa someday.

What did most of these young people think of Mandela, whose face they had never seen? All they knew were stories of his exploits in the 1950s when he publicly burned his ID pass, and when he sparked resistance movements by being the first black man to deliberately trespass in places reserved for whites. Mandela was the man who demanded that the white power structure enter into negotiations. But these young people, many of them children, had no thought of negotiations. They were ready to throw bombs and shoot bullets. Even Mandela had agreed to the use of bombs for the purpose of sabotage. The first one was exploded by Umkhonto we Sizwe in December of 1961.

When Mandela saw these youths arriving as prisoners at Robben Island he was amazed, almost shocked, by their behavior. "They refused to follow the most basic prison rules," he wrote. "One day I was speaking with the warden in his office. As we both walked out we noticed a prisoner being interrogated by an officer. [...] The warden said to this young man, 'Take off your hat, please.' The prisoner turned around to face the warden, and said: 'Why?' I couldn't believe my ears. 'Because it's against the rules,' the warden replied.

And the young man answered, 'Why is it against the rules? What's the reason for a rule like that?'"

Mandela and his friends would have to learn great patience in dealing with these young men. They learned to listen sympathetically to these angry emissaries of a new era, a generation of which they knew little. This was the only way a dialogue of mutual respect could begin.

Nevertheless, in all the black ghettos outside the prison walls, in all the camps of the liberation armies outside the country, and in all the cities of exile from London to Moscow, the name Mandela meant freedom. Robben Island became known as "Mandela University." This was partly because the prisoners there were actively encouraged by him to study law and political history; but it was also because the heartbeat of the revolution was there. It was not long before having been to prison at Robben Island became both an honor and a sort of status symbol of initiation. Having been there meant having been close to the great man. It was quite rare that this actually occurred, since the prisoners of the so-called "Rivonia" group were segregated as much as possible from the others. A man might have spent years in the same prison as Mandela without ever catching a glimpse of him. Even so, the symbolic power of having been in the same prison was undiminished.

Makana

This tradition found its first public expression in a short story entitled, *A Pilgrimage to the Isle of Makana,* by a black South African writer named Mtutuzeli Matshoba.[3] A young black man working in Johannesburg receives long-awaited leave to go on a kind of pilgrimage, which in this case signifies a visit to see his imprisoned brother at Robben Island. "And will you also see *him* ?" his friends ask.

---

[3] The story is part of the author's collection *Call Me Not a Man* (Johannesburg: Ravan Press, 1979).

After the long voyage from Johannesburg to the Cape, filled with unexpected encounters and events, he finally crosses the stretch of sea in a small boat and lands on the Island.

> Although light and hesitant, my first step onto the Isle of Makana came as a shock to my entire being. For me this ground was as sacred as my ancestors' kraal, where no one had the right to set foot, except for the holy ones.

Then, after speaking for half an hour with his brother, the pilgrim returns to the boat which takes him back to Cape Town. As he watches the Island diminish in the distance, he wonders:

> Where might one find Nelson Mandela on the Isle? Certainly not among the other sons of Africa. Blessed Mandela! Have they decided to let him die slowly on this island? Have they any inkling of his place in the inner sanctum of the hearts of many a black African? Did they imagine we might forget him and his companions if they banished him to this island? And did they imagine we could forget the misery of our lives?

Makana was a Xhosa holy man who distinguished himself in 1819 during a war against the whites.

> The Africans' reaction to the military defeats, the loss of lands, the ever-growing white population pressure, as well as the inroads of churches and Christian schools, was to seek supernatural help. The Xhosas turned toward their ancestors. They listened to oracles and prophets.
>
> In 1819 Makana (or Nxele), a soothsayer, attacked the city of Grahamstown, leading 10,000 men. The attack failed and he was taken prisoner. The people waited long for his return, but it turned out that he was drowned while trying to escape from Robben Island in 1820.[4]

---

[4] Monica Wilson and Leonard Thompson, *A History of South Africa* (Cape Town-Johannesburg: David Philip Publishers, 1982).

Nelson Mandela, himself a Xhosa, had written of Nxele: "His memory lives on in the language of my people. They still use the term *Ukuza kuka Nxele* to mean 'shattered hopes.'"

In Mtutuzeli Matshoba's short story the meaning of the linking of Makana with Mandela is clear. The latter takes his place in the long history of the African struggle against European colonization. The Isle becomes both a mythic and a historical place; and the historical roots of the Mandela myth become clear.

When the white rulers decided in 1964 to send Nelson Mandela to the penitentiary at Robben Island they became unwitting players in the long African saga of struggle symbolized by that place. Perhaps they were ignorant of its aura of symbolic power in the people's imagination. But whether they liked it or not the Island made them the current villains in the great South African story of struggle against white invasion—a story that went all the way back to the Cape colony governors of the Dutch East India Company, as well as to the British crown later on.

By the same token, Nelson Mandela became the spiritual heir of all the heroic chieftains who had resisted this inexorable force of colonialism, often with vastly inferior weaponry and numbers, against the European armies. The National Party, which had been in power since 1948, made no secret of the nature of its struggle: first, against the indigenous African majority; second, against the British influence. Apartheid was a final desperate attempt to reverse the momentum of this history, and to enforce their fantasy of the country's Afrikaner past. Mandela's great strength was that he was one of the first eminent Africans to make use of this mythic drama of African emancipation with modern skills and perspectives.

This is why the act of locking him up on Robben Island seemed almost like an anachronism, a mythic act in itself. It would nourish the image of Mandela as sacred liberator, helping to create a new myth that would become more powerful than all the prisons, police forces, and armies. If the authorities had decided to keep him in a modern prison with no such history (the maximum security facility at Pretoria,[5] for example), the Mandela story might have had a different outcome.

A Descendant of Kings

Another fact which was never really understood by the white authorities was the symbolic power, for black South Africans, of Nelson Mandela's own family origins. He was seen as the new Makana, not only because he was a Xhosa, but because he was a descendent of the royal family, which had always been one of the most powerful Xhosa tribes, the Thembus. His royal genealogy goes back to the sixteenth century.

This noble ancestry played its role in legitimizing his leadership of the ANC. In the collective consciousness of South African blacks, the modern struggle against apartheid and for full emancipation has deep roots in the struggle of Africans against European invaders, ever since they landed at the Cape in 1652.

Nelson Mandela's charismatic power lies in his ability to combine ancient and modern values. On the one hand, his membership in a royal family of the Thembu; and on the other, his successful studies in history and law—first at Fort Hare University for blacks, then in Johannesburg. His royal, warrior ancestry, plus his profession as lawyer, gave him a towering and incontestable authority. Of course there was more to him than this. No amount of charisma could have substituted for the extraordinary skill and political insight he showed as activist and political leader. One might summarize this by saying that he had three major facets: member of the Xhosa nobility; lawyer; and activist leader. In the eyes of those youth who referred to Robben Island as "Mandela University" he was the exemplary modern African leader.

Because of its bondage to the past, Afrikaner power never understood these dimensions of Nelson Mandela's personality.

---

[5] Breyten Breytenbach, *The True Confessions of an Albino Terrorist* (New York: Farrar, Strauss, Giroux, 1984).

From 1964 on, not one of the leaders of white power understood that Mandela was something more than a mere political figure. Trying to make his image disappear only nourished the secret strength of that which they were trying to destroy.

At the end of the film *Viva Zapata,* by Elia Kazan, the soldiers who had killed Zapata in an ambush exhibited his corpse near a village. Peasants came to look at it. However, the people pretended not to recognize the body. They expressed the belief that he was still alive, and in fact immortal. This recalls the symbol of Zapata's white horse, that had escaped the massacre and is still said to haunt the surrounding mountains.

This is how myths begin. They are virtually indestructible because they do not depend merely on concrete facts. They live simultaneously in the collective imagination of a people and in the most intimate dreams of the men and women who are its members.

The myth of Nelson Mandela truly came into its own when the authorities attempted to make him disappear behind the walls of the penitentiary. They simply could not understand that Mandela was far more than a political adversary, or even a revolutionary. He belonged to that rare category of human beings whose personal destiny is bound up with the history and destiny of a people. Thus his imprisonment and "disappearance" only reinforced the power of his image. When the private individual is eclipsed the idea and the myth remain, and may become even more powerful.

This book covers the formative years of Nelson Mandela's life (from 1918 to 1943). It emphasizes the dual cultural background of South Africa's greatest president: his royal ancestry in the context of rural, traditional African life; and his university education and professional training in the context of modern urban life.

The Transkei, near the Bashee River—Nelson Mandela's native land.

Herds of cattle, with the village of Qunu in the distance.

Passage Through Smoke

It was cold at Mvezo on that early Thursday morning of July 18, 1918. According to the Xhosa calendar, it was the "month of aloe." The winter cold is not severe in this area of the Transkei, except during times of the "high wind," as they call it, when the north wind sweeps down from the Stormberg and Drakensberg mountains, gusting through the hills. The Indian Ocean is only forty miles away, and the weather is often misty and humid. The breath of the vast herds of cattle on the prairies sends up a visible steam.

Henry Gadla Mphakanyiswa, chief of Mvezo village, lowered his head in order to step out of the hut of his third wife, Nosekeni, daughter of Nkedama, of the Mpenvu clan. Chiefs—or for that matter any men in that society—were allowed as many wives as they wished, provided they could pay the *lobola*, the traditional dowry measured in heads of livestock. Each wife then took charge of her own household and children according to a precise ranking system which determined both social role and inheritance.

In a polygamous family such as that of Henry Mphakanyiswa, the husband is expected to make regular visits to his wives, called "counting the huts." This term refers to the successive periods during which the father lives with each family, according to a specific calendar. A typical example might be a week or a month with the wife of the largest house, the same period with the wife of "the right hand," and so on down the line, until each wife has received her due.

So it was that Nelson Mandela, like many other children of the Transkei, was accustomed from infancy to seeing his father for only a week out of each month. These long absences added to the paternal mystique and authority.

Nosekeni had just given birth to her first child, a boy. The total number of children born to Henry Mphakanyiswa and his four wives reached thirteen. This was the youngest of his four sons, who would later have two sisters.

In their round hut, several yards in diameter, the thatched roof was supported by a central pillar. That morning, an elderly midwife and herbal healer had Nosekeni drink a potion of medicinal roots and marine gorse to calm her and improve her circulation. After washing the newborn child, she had him drink a few drops of a mixture made from juniper berries, which would give him good health. Then she used a small stick to spread a paste made from aloe juice over the umbilical cord near the navel. She repeated this process until the cord withered and broke free. Then she went to bury the placenta behind the huts.

The midwife also placed some of this paste under the baby's nostrils, so as to get rid of excess mucus. She used it to clean his ears as well. Then she hung a piece of tree euphorbia on the wall of the hut above the newborn, who lay wrapped in his blanket. Nosekeni had dug this plant up before she went into labor. It was a charm to keep away all evil, and especially disease.

When all of these rituals had been completed, the father reentered the hut and lit a small fire on the ground to the left of the entrance, near Nosekeni, an area reserved for women. He waited until the fire was going strong before he placed some green twigs that he had cut that morning upon the coals. This generated clouds of thick, pungent smoke. The mother then took the baby, holding his legs in one hand and his hands in the other, and passed him through the smoke, swinging him gently, humming softly, and turning him to be sure that his entire body came into contact with the smoke.

The local Christian missionaries considered this "passage through smoke" a form of baptism by fire. But this is clearly a cultural projection. For one thing, there is no notion in Bantu culture corresponding to the Christian doctrine of a fault, or original sin, which is purified through baptism. The passage through smoke is a rite of protection, not of purification. Furthermore, the southern African conception of the spiritual nature of water is very different from that of European culture, whether Christian or pagan. In Western cultures, water, especially coming from springs, is most often the abode or haunt of benevolent and protective spirits. But in the Transkei, where the hills abound in rivers, creeks, and streams that flow down from the mountains, people fear water spirits such as Tikoloshe, Hili, and Dziyana. They are believed to cause all kinds of harm.

However, it was not water spirits, but more mundane social forces that were sowing discord behind the scenes of this boy's life. On May 31, 1910, eight years before Rolihlahla's birth, the colony of South Africa became the Union of South Africa. This was a federation, under British dominion, of the provinces of the Cape, of Natal, and of the older Boer republics of Transvaal and the Orange Free State. This date was not arbitrary, for it had also been on May 31, 1902 that the Vereeniging treaty was signed, ending the famous Boer War, that had begun in October 1899. The British, who had conquered the Cape colony in 1815, later made the mistake in 1850 of granting sovereignty to the Boer republics of Transvaal and Orange. They had satisfied themselves with gaining control of the Kimberley diamond mines. Yet only three decades would pass before the discovery in the Transvaal, in 1886, of one of the largest gold lodes in the world. After an unsuccessful attempt to annex this new El Dorado, Britain went to war in the last year of the century. The terrible Boer War that resulted was, in several respects, a forerunner of the atrocities of twentieth-century warfare: contempt for human rights, and the first military use of trenches, barbed wire, and concentration camps.

Beginning with their defeat and subjugation by the British in 1902, the Boers (i.e., Afrikaners) became obsessed with recovering their autonomy and gaining independence.

This process would finally be completed over half a century later. In 1961, it was again the symbolic date and place of May 31, at Vereeniging, that made headlines. The Afrikaners (who had taken over political power in 1948) resigned from the Commonwealth and declared the independence of the Republic of South Africa.

Hence the creation of the Union of South Africa in 1910 was but the first step in the journey toward independence from Britain. It was on that date that the country came under the rule of an autonomous government and parliament, chosen by "free and democratic" elections. Of course, this freedom and democracy did not include blacks. Only a few who lived in Cape Province and owned land could vote. Even this small exception, known as a "franchise," would be gradually eliminated in the years to come.

As soon as this new political situation became stabilized, three laws were passed that clearly showed the intentions of those presently in power. The first, voted in 1911, was the Native Labour Regulation Act. It declared that any "natives"—meaning all persons of African or mixed blood—who quit their jobs for reasons of their own were in violation of the law and subject to penalties. The second law, also voted in 1911, was the Mines and Works Act. This instituted the first formal racial barriers in work, by declaring certain types of employment as reserved for whites. Finally, there was the Native Land Act of 1913, which prohibited non-whites from owning more than 7.3 percent of the land in South Africa. The remaining 92.7 percent of the land was reserved for whites. This law was important for the future development of white power and had three objectives. First, it protected Afrikaner farmers who felt threatened by black farming; and they had reason to feel threatened: between 1910 and 1912, indigenous Africans had succeeded in buying seventy-eight farms, often through cooperatives. This movement portended a future of black integration into the economy. The 1913 law put a brutal stop to this. Another intentional effect of the law was forced urbanization of large black populations, which would provide cheap labor for mines and industries. In combination with the first two laws, depriving blacks of basic workers' rights, it guaranteed a huge, permanent, cheap, low-skilled labor force that could be exploited at will in the white-owned economy.

However, the resulting rural exodus of blacks became so huge that white urban workers ultimately began to feel threatened in their turn. They began a series of major strikes in 1913 to obtain strict enforcement of racial segregation in work. They finally won their cause in 1922, after violent strikes that bordered on insurrection. The government had to resort to using the army to subdue the strikers, who went so far as to dig themselves into trenches.

But the effects of the land laws went much further than simply protecting white farmers and creating a black labor pool for industry. They also formed the foundation of apartheid society. This became explicit in 1948 with the creation of the "homelands." Apartheid required that all South Africans be formally identified according to their racial origin (White, Mixed, Indian, or Black), and then their cultural and linguistic origin (Xhosa, Zulu, etc....). Each black was associated with a specific "homeland," which he or she was supposed to be a citizen of, and which would supposedly become independent someday. The 1913 law had defined 264 reservations which covered 7.3 percent of South African territory, and were based on old British reservations of the last century. This total area was magnanimously increased to 13.7 percent in 1936. The problem, of course, was that it had to somehow accommodate 70 percent of the country's population! Beginning in 1948, these 264 parcels were regrouped into ten homelands. These were not contiguous areas, but bits and pieces which were not coveted by whites. Thus there were forty-eight separate parcels for the Zulus, nineteen for the Botswana people, and four for the Transkei tribes. If apartheid had really achieved its own pretended objectives, these

ten homelands would long ago have become independent countries, and blacks would have lost their South African citizenship
and become foreign migrant workers from their own homeland
countries. As it turned out, when apartheid was abolished in 1990,
four of these homelands (including the Transkei) did attain a form
of autonomy.

Hence the Land Act of 1913, enacted five years before Nelson
Mandela's birth, must be seen as a crucial transition point, leading
from the colonial period of the nineteenth century to the apartheid
system of the twentieth. Far from implying a breach between these
eras, it actually provided a logical and consistent continuity.
Apartheid could arguably be considered a form of modern colonialism. However, the process involved a kind of reverse colonization, since it was the colonial power which withdrew and its former
subjects who now colonized.

This important decade also saw the creation of political parties and organizations whose influence would be decisive in twentieth-century South African history. In 1912, in Bloemfontein, right
in the Afrikaner bastion of the Orange Free State, a black organization known as the African Native National Congress was formed.
In 1923, it would become the famous African National Congress,
or ANC.

Two years later, General Hertzog founded the National Party,
with the slogan "South Africa first!" Of course, it was clear that this
really meant Afrikaners first. Its platform text declared: "As concerns our attitude towards the natives, our fundamental principle
is that of the superiority of European peoples, in a spirit of Christian paternalism. We absolutely reject any attempts at race-mixing."

The National Party took power in 1948. Its main adversary would
turn out to be the ANC. These two organizations were destined
to become the major forces in South African political life, with Nelson Mandela as one of the main actors.

A third organization was created on June 5, 1918, only a month
before the birth of Rolihlahla Madiba: the Broederbond ("the

Brotherhood"). This was a secret society that admitted only Afrikaners. Its goal was to stop at nothing to ensure a South Africa dominated by white Christian Afrikaners. From 1948 until 1990, every prime minister and every president was a member of the Broederbond. It was this organization that invented the system of apartheid.

It would seem that all the major forces had taken form by the end of the first decade after the creation of the Union of South Africa. In a sense, the stage was already set for Rolihlahla Madiba to play his historic role thirty years later, as Nelson Mandela.

One of his first decisive allies was a man who would have a major influence on the young Nelson when he arrived in Johannesburg in 1942: Walter Max Ulyate Sisulu. He was born in 1912, six years before Rolihlahla, at Engcobo in the northern Transkei. Another essential character in Mandela's life was Oliver Reginald Tambo, born in 1917 in Bizana, in the far eastern region of the Transkei, near the Natal border.[6] Mandela first became friends with Tambo in 1940 at the university for blacks at Fort Hare. They would meet again in Johannesburg through the ANC's Youth League, and would work together to create South Africa's first black law offices in 1953.

When we consider that Hendrik Verwoerd (prime minister in 1964 when Mandela was sentenced, and generally considered the "architect of apartheid") was born in 1910,[7] and that his successor, John Vorster, was born in 1915, we may conclude that all the major players in the portentous events of 1948 were already alive when Rolihlahla Madiba was born in July, 1918.

---

[6] Winnie Mandela (Nomzamo Zamiewe Winnifred Madikizela), whom Mandela married in 1958, was also a native of Bizana. Evelyne Ntoko Mase, his first wife, from Engcobo, was related to the Sisulu family.

[7] Verwoerd was actually born in the Netherlands, but his family emigrated to South Africa in 1903.

When Mandela was two weeks old, Nosekeni tied a belt around his waist, called the *um-kwinti*, after a species of tree. Shortly before the baby was born, Nosekeni had used the veins of this tree's large leaves to weave a supple cord which would not irritate his skin. Adjustable exactly to his size, the belt provided a means of keeping track of his growth. If it seemed too large after several days, it meant that the baby was not being fed enough. And if it had to be made longer, all was judged to be well.

As in many other cultures, the naming of the baby was a very important affair. For boys, this right was reserved for the father. For girls, the mother chose the name, though the father's opinion was taken into account. In some cases a long time would elapse— up to a year or two after birth—before a first name was finally chosen. Meanwhile, the child would be called *Ntamekana,* meaning "little one," or "Junior." The name might be chosen according to the child's position in the family ("the Inheritor," for example), or perhaps because of some external circumstance surrounding the birth (for example, a child might be named the Xhosa equivalent of "Magistrate" if a white administrator happened to arrive at the time of birth). The name might also be inspired by some celestial event, such as the passage of a comet. Or it might simply refer to some physical or psychological characteristic attributed to the child (for example, *Matanzima,* meaning "thick saliva").

Could it be that Nosekeni's son showed a turbulent character early on? Did he create special problems for those around him? It must have been something like this that inspired Henry Gadla Mphakanyiswa to choose the unusual name Rolihlahla,[8] meaning "creator of problems." In his autobiography,[9] written at the age

---

[8] The *h* in this name signifies a type of click which is typical of a number of southern African languages. There is no equivalent in any Indo-European language. Xhosa has three types of click consonants, transcribed by the letters *h*, *g*, and *q*.

[9] *Long Walk to Freedom* (New York: Little, Brown & Co., 1995).

of seventy-six, South Africa's first black president speaks with amusement of this name: "I don't believe that a name decides a destiny, nor that my father somehow foresaw my future. But later on my friends and relatives would jokingly attribute to my name the many storms which I let loose and endured."

A Thembu Chieftain's Name

Rolihlahla Madiba is Nelson Mandela's real, original Xhosa name. Madiba is the name of his clan, after a famous Thembu chieftain ancestor who lived at the end of the seventeenth century, before the European conquest.

But Rolihlahla Madiba was also a member of a special royal family within the Thembu tribe. This is a lineage of traditional chiefs who became allied with British colonial power. Both the British rulers of the nineteenth century and the South African whites who came into power after 1910 relied on such chiefs to govern the country. So it was that behind every local white administrator, known as a magistrate, or commissioner, there was a black traditional chief who exercised direct power. After 1948, Afrikaner power cleverly attempted to enlist these chiefs as their allies in the politics of apartheid, whose ultimate goal was to exclude blacks from most of South Africa, banishing them to "independent" homelands, which would then be given to these traditional royal families to rule in exchange for their cooperation.

This actually succeeded with the Transkei's independence in 1976, ruled by the Matanzima branch of the tribe. Like Rolihlahla Madiba, they were descendants of the great Thembu King, Ngubengenka, who ruled from 1809 until his death in 1832. In fact, this royal family's genealogy goes back the early seventeenth century, to King Dlomo, second son of Nxego, who reigned in 1600. Nxego himself was a descendent of the very first of the

Thembu Kings, Zwide, who is reported to have reigned around the end of the fifteenth century.

These reports come from shipwrecked sailors who were able to reach the coast in smaller boats. Some of the earliest stories are those of Portuguese sailors who escaped the wreck of the *São João* in June, 1552, landing in the northern Transkei. These men walked up the coast, covering over 300 miles, meeting up with the explorer Lourenço Marques at what is now known as Maputo. During their long walk, they encountered a number of coastal peoples and made notes about their customs and chiefs. As the number of European travelers, especially English and Dutch, began to increase in the area during the seventeenth century, shipwreck survivors became more common. Some of them settled down to live with the Africans. For example, in 1635, the survivors of the *Belem* discovered a white man living in the Transkei who had himself survived the sinking of the *Santo Alberto* off the coast near Umtata in 1593—over forty years prior! This man had been only a cabin boy at the time when he was abandoned by the other sailors because he appeared to be fatally ill. Now he had three wives, many children, and a huge herd of livestock. In February 1686, a Dutch ship, the *Stavenisse,* sank about sixty miles south of what is now Durban. Among the large number of survivors, forty-seven men decided to walk back to Cape Town—over 560 miles away! They made it to the Bay of Natal (now Durban), where they found other shipwreck survivors. They then built a ship, the *Centaurus,* and discovered eighteen sailors living near the mouth of the Kei River, in the southern Transkei. Some months later another ship picked up the remaining survivors. All these wanderings along the coast, and to some extent inland, resulted in much information about indigenous peoples. When we combine these nautical memoirs with those of later missionaries, explorers, and traders, a fairly accurate picture of royal genealogies can be reconstructed. Of course, this only applies to coastal areas, and therefore to the ancestral homelands of Mandela's tribe, the royal Thembus of the Transkei.

At the beginning of the twentieth century, the white authorities set up district councils in the Transkei. These were supposed to resolve "native" problems, and were of course headed by the traditional chiefs. In 1929, these councils were all brought into a single organization, the United General Council of the Transkei, more familiarly known as the Bunga.

When Rolihlahla was only eleven years old, his second father was appointed regent over the Thembu tribe. This man, Jongintaba, second son of Dalindyebo, had adopted the young Rolihlahla after he had become an orphan two years earlier. On this special occasion of the establishment of the Bunga at Umtata, the new Regent brought his own son, Justice, as well as his adoptive son. Thus Mandela was quite young when he got his first glimpse of the pomp and ceremony of white power, which was displayed lavishly on this occasion so as to impress the Africans.

W.T. Brownlee, the white governor of the Transkei, was the son of Charles Brownlee, a missionary from the English colony of the late nineteenth century. In his book, *Reminiscence of a Transkeian,* he describes the installation of the Bunga. He gives the names of the chiefs seated before him, among them the young Rolihlahla.

> The representatives of the nations and tribes of the territories were all gathered in this great hall. The sons of Thembu[10] were there, the sons of Dlomo, of Ngubengcuka, of Mtirara, and those of the house of Janse, the sacred bull of Dalindyebo, all direct descendants of the first chief, called Zwide.[11]

This royal ancestry would play a decisive role in the destiny of the wonderstruck young boy sitting there. However, it is significant that he did not belong to a ruling branch of the family. The polygamous system of ranking of wives operated at all levels, from the King of the Xhosas to Thembu nobles, including Rolihlahla's family.

[10] "Tembu" was also the name of one of the earliest Tembu kings of the sixteenth century.

[11] See Mandela's genealogical chart at the end of the book.

His father was a very minor chief, a simple advisor to the King. His own first wife managed the "Big House," with the second and third wives managing the "right-hand" and "left-hand" houses, respectively. Through his grandmother Simhkade, and his grandfather Mandela, Rolihlahla belonged to the Ixhiba, the lowest-ranking family in the royal hierarchy. Neither he nor his father had any prospect of attaining the throne.

The Cape Town authorities had appointed Henry Gadla Mphakanyiswa as chief of Mvezo. He received a modest salary for this, as well as a percentage of the various taxes. He was a very tall man, with dark skin and "an imposing bearing," as his son later wrote. Mandela also remembers his father as having a lock of white hair which sometimes hung down on his forehead. When Nelson's own face was revealed to the world after his release from prison in 1990, people saw a tall man with imposing bearing, and a very similar lock of white hair over his forehead—a lock that would become blended in with totally white hair in the years to come.

Relations between white petty officials and the traditional chiefs were often strained. The former, invested in their belief in their European racial superiority, spoke as governors. The chiefs, conscious of their own African ancestry, easily took offense at this. Although he was only the chief of a small village, Henry Gadla had been advisor to two Thembu Kings: Dalindybo (died in 1920), and Jongilizwe (died in 1926); he later became advisor to the Regent Jongintaba.

One day, when two-year-old Rolihlahla was playing in the dust in front of his mother's hut, a black messenger from the local white administrator arrived, looking for his father. Henry Gadla was there in the village tending to the animals in the kraal. After reading the message, he rejected it angrily. This resulted in his being summoned to appear immediately before the white administrator himself.

Henry Gadla refused to go. His anger was partly due to the disrespectful tone of the letter, but it was mostly because the matter in question was none of the white authorities' business. A cow had escaped from a meadow, and the problem was one which concerned only Thembus. It was up to him, and only him, to resolve this matter. He was Chief of Mvezo and advisor to the Regent, Jongintaba. He told the messenger that he refused to go to the white administrator, and that he would challenge the man to a fight, if necessary. For anyone acquainted with the local culture, this was not a provocation to violence, but a ritual formula, traditionally used to express total refusal.

Sixty years later, Nelson Mandela would speak of these events, defending his father from that legal perspective which was his lifelong forte: "This challenge was not a manifestation of bad temper, but a question of principle," he wrote.

But the minor white official didn't see it that way. Taking the law into his own hands, he deposed the traditional chief. From one day to the next, Henry Gadla found himself deprived of his title and revenues, and in a quandary as to how to feed his four families.

Nosekeni was obliged to leave Mvezo for Qunu, a village only a few miles away. Larger than Mvezo, it bordered the east-west road through the Transkei (today a major highway). She wore her most beautiful, vividly colored dress, and a huge black-and-white turban on her head. Rolihlahla was strapped onto her back in a long band of cloth wrapped around his chest. He was used to being carried like this, and easily fell asleep to the rhythm of Nosekeni's walk and the lullaby she was singing:

> *Sleep, sleep my baby,*
> *Sleep, sleep little Rolihlahla,*
> *Sleep, sleep my little frog,*
> *Sleep, sleep my little lamb,*
> *Sleep, sleep my little darling,*
> *Sway along with me,*
> *For your mother has a long way to walk to Qunu.*[12]

---

[12] The last line of this familiar lullaby would vary according to what Nosekeni was doing: i.e., "For your mother must harvest the pumpkins," or "For your mother is gathering wood."

Qunu had about a hundred inhabitants, mostly women, children, and the elderly. Most of the young men had left to work in the gold mines of Johannesburg.

It was surrounded by a uniform landscape of green, grassy hills with very few trees, but vast herds of animals. These were accompanied by many white birds, who sat on the backs of cattle and rid them of their parasites. Today, on the other side of the highway, there is a small wooded area called Qunu Forest.

Nosekeni built her own kraal in the western end of the village. This was a traditional grouping of three round straw huts with conical thatched roofs, with a corral for the animals and a small garden where she would grow corn, beans, and pumpkins. The Dutch word *kraal* originally had the same meaning as its English cognate "corral," but in South Africa it had come to include the whole ensemble of huts and garden; sometimes it was expanded to refer to the village itself, and also to one's place of origin.

Nosekeni built the corral itself first. She drove wooden stakes into the ground and linked them with loosely woven reeds. This fence was completed by adding thorny branches and even entire bushes to prevent cattle from escaping and predators from entering. A few yards away she traced the outlines of the three round huts, arranging them in a semicircle. The space between them and the entrance of the corral formed a kind of family courtyard.

The two-and-a-half-year-old Rolihlahla looked on as his mother, helped by her husband and his other wives, erected the walls of the huts. The women made a frame of reeds and set it in the ground. When everything else was ready, they covered it on both sides with a kind of adobe. The resulting wall was about a foot thick and six feet high. Its only openings were one window and a low door, less than five feet high. Adults had to stoop to enter it. This door faced east, following ancient custom. Henry Gadla set a central pillar to support the roof, which was made of gorse branches woven together with vines known as "monkey rope." Also following tradition, he inserted the bulb of a lily-like flower into the thatched wall as a protection from lightning.

The Xhosa have a dread of lightning, which is sent by the Thunderbird, whose home is in the sky. Some tales about huts struck by lightning even claim that feathers were found at the scene, and are preserved by shamans as power objects.

When lightning strikes a human being, animal, or home, a shaman is summoned to treat the person or animal, and especially to rid the place of the harmful influence which entered into the earth there. If someone is killed by lightning, the shaman summons all the members of the family, making scars on certain parts of their bodies and then applying herbal remedies to these areas. He also covers their upper bodies from the forehead down to the shoulders and arms with a potion made from sweat. Then the men must dig a deep grave and bury the deceased, wrapping them well, so that the body does not come into direct contact with the earth. All the objects which they were carrying at the time must be buried with them. In the case of an animal, the body is hacked to pieces before it is buried.

At the place where the lightning entered the ground, it is said that there is sometimes a small egg similar to that of a chicken.

> In a sense, thunderbolts are as eternal as the mountains. The Thunderbird lays its egg in the depths of the earth. When its time has come, it hatches open in the darkness, drawing fire back into the earth, a fire which chars and burns away all that is superfluous, so that life can spring forth anew, giving red flowers, grasses and bushes, and all that grows. Like life in the mother's womb, the Thunderbird's egg waits in the darkness for the moment of birth.[13]

---

[13] André Brink, *A Chain of Voices* (New York: Viking Penguin, 1989). The character who is speaking here is a slave who starts a revolt. André Brink reverses the traditional myth of the Thunderbird, regarded as malevolent by the Xhosa, making it into the destructive but liberating fire of revolution.

Inside her new home, Nosekeni pounded down the earth, then covered the floor with fine powdery soil from anthills, mixed with fresh cow dung. When it dries, this compound becomes very hard, and provides a solid, even floor that can easily be swept clean.

From that day on, Rolihlahla, his mother, and sisters began to sleep on mats in the central hut, in the customary position with head resting on elbow. The area to the left of the entrance was reserved for girls and women. There was no furniture. At night, the door and window were carefully shut to protect the family from the water spirits—and probably from the summer mosquitoes and winter cold as well.

The next hut to the right was Nosekeni's kitchen. When the weather was good, she would build a fire outside and set a kettle with three legs upon the hearth. It may have contained corn soup or milk. Otherwise, she would cook inside the kitchen hut. The iron kettle was set upon a fire burning in a hole in the center of the hut. The smoke escaped through a round hole in the roof. But the door or window had to be left open in order maintain a draft, so that the hut would not become so filled with smoke that it would become hard to breathe. The family ate their meals on the ground, using their hands to take food from the communal platter. Most of the time the men formed one circle around their platter, and the women another around theirs.

The third hut was the pantry, where Nosekeni kept the corn she harvested from her fields (a type of maize from India, whose ears are called "mealies"), as well as millet, beans (red, black, and pinto), and a kind of lentil. Because of the absence of good ventilation and protection from humidity, the food was sometimes poorly preserved here, and lost to mold and weevils.

The harvests were mostly meager. In the nineteenth century, the European plow and iron hoe were introduced in the Transkei. Because of the high price of plows, the Xhosas mostly had to use hoes for many years. Beginning in 1902, after the Boer War was over, a type of plow called the "American 75," with an iron blade and a wooden handle, became more available to African farmers. By the time Rolihlahla was born, iron plows were widely used.

But the shortage of selectively bred seeds made harvests difficult. Nosekeni tried to select out the best-looking seeds from those she kept. She would test a batch by throwing a handful onto the upturned lid of a kettle which was placed on the fire. If the grains of corn or beans popped with a sharp sound, it meant that the batch they came from had been protected from the humidity and could be planted. The children were then allowed to eat the popped grains as a special treat.

In 1990, my wife and I made a trip to Qunu. Nelson Mandela was still in prison, but the rumor was out that he would soon be free. At that time it was still a small traditional village which sat beside National Highway 2. There were several dozen round huts with earthen walls and conical thatched roofs. A few roofs were made of tin. There were also several rectangular brick houses with corrugated metal roofs, a very widespread style in small towns in South Africa, even among some of the well-to-do whites.

We were shown three circular traces, barely visible on the grassy ground. These were all that remained of Nosekeni's huts, where Rolihlahla lived from early childhood until he was nine years old. It felt like an entire world had vanished. Pondering these traces as if they were indecipherable hieroglyphs, I was somehow reminded of the ruins of the town of Thurii in southern Italy. Those traces were barely more visible than these. The town had been built by the companions of Spartacus, leader of the great slave revolt. They had left their homes almost two thousand years ago to go into battle against the Roman army, and never returned. Now all that remained of the walls were chunks of ineradicable brown clay imbedded in the earth, the silent witnesses, like Nosekeni's enchanted circles, of a vanished life.

We were also shown a field, a large grassy meadow whose borders were hard to distinguish. This was "Mandela's field." One day, it was said, he would return here and build his house.

I never returned to Qunu, but I learned years later from Daryl Evans, who had taken photographs there in 1996, that Nelson Mandela had in fact built a house near there—a substantial one this time. However, he did not build it on "Mandela's field," but on the other side of the highway.

It is a exact copy of the house inside the walls of Victor Vester Prison at Paarl, where the world's most famous political prisoner spent his last months in captivity. It has a vast living room, three bedrooms, and a large kitchen. As Mandela himself said, the house at Victor Vester was "a halfway-house between prison and freedom. The idyllic scene is marred only by the barbed wire on top of the outer walls, and the guards at the entrance."

In Qunu itself, there are no guards (though security personnel surely keep a sharp eye on things). The only barbed wire is that which fences in certain fields, and which does not always succeed in its purpose of keeping the animals from straying. Otherwise, the open country of green hills around the village has scarcely changed since the child who would become the country's greatest president lived there.

A Path Laid Out by Their Fathers

The first world that Rolihlahla discovered was bounded by the Transkei hills. It was a traditional society in which each new generation was shaped by custom, ritual, and taboo. Of course, he was too young to realize that his society was in the throes of an upheaval that had begun a century earlier. "Men followed the path laid out by their fathers; and women led the same lives as their mothers before them," he later wrote. This expresses his own childhood view, for new generations are rarely aware of the extent to which they live in change.

Modern South African history begins with a shipwreck—one which had far-reaching repercussions. In 1647, the *Harlem*, a ship belonging to the Dutch East India Company, sank in a storm off Table Bay. It was laden with spices from the Dutch colony of Batavia in the East Indies (now Jakarta in Indonesia), and was bound for the Netherlands. In addition to the dangerous weather, this was a very hard voyage for sailors in those days. According to the season, they had to spend from five to seven months without going ashore. The island of Saint Helena was the only port available to the Dutch at this time. On this occasion, typical of such voyages, all the wild goats and pigs had long been slaughtered and there was no more fresh meat to be had.

Survivors from the *Harlem* reached the coast at the place where Cape Town was later founded. They spent a year there, waiting to be spotted by a passing ship. They found a fertile country with abundant rain, a Mediterranean climate, and no cannibals (a major bugaboo for Europeans of that era). When they finally returned to Holland, they submitted a report to the "Seventeen," as the executive council of the Dutch East India Company was known. This report was in effect a complaint to the council, demanding that future voyages include a stop at the Cape.

Twenty months later, on March 20, 1651, the Seventeen finally accepted a recommendation to that effect from several different committees. "In order for ships sailing between the Netherlands and Batavia to procure fresh water, vegetables, meat, and other such necessities, as well as to care for the sick, a supply port shall be established at the Cape of Good Hope."

On April 7, 1652, a battalion of ninety men, led by Jan van Riebeeck, landed at the foot of Table Mountain. Van Riebeeck's mission was to built a fort on the banks of the river which flowed into the sea there, and to plant crops and provide pasturage for livestock there. The latter were to be bought from the local natives, whom the shipwrecked crew had found to be hospitable.

When van Riebeeck finally left the Cape ten years later, his mission was achieved. The new port settlement was receiving ships from the Company[14] and furnishing them with vital necessities for their voyages. One might suppose that this was how the story of the South African colony began. But the facts proved to be quite otherwise.

Until the end of the eighteenth century, and the dissolution of the Dutch East India Company in 1794, there were two opposing forces at work. The first was the Company itself, which had absolutely no desire to establish a colony. Its only interest in the Cape was to have a supply port for its ships. In sharp contrast to this were the aspirations of the overseas employees of the Company. Most of them were wretchedly poor and had no desire to return to Europe, where they had no prospects of employment after their service was completed. Little by little, and despite great

---

[14] About fifty per year until the end of the eighteenth century.

managerial reluctance, they succeeded in settling on farms rented to them by the Company. The true colonists (in the strict sense of the term, those who arrived directly from Europe) were actually small in number, in spite of the demand, and in spite of certain official declarations of the necessity of colonizing the Cape. The 200 French Protestants who were sent in 1688, after the revocation of the Edict of Nantes, represented perhaps the only major effort at colonization of that era.

This situation changed at the end of the eighteenth century. Almost as many slaves had been imported from Mozambique, Angola, West Africa, and Malaysia as had colonists. In 1778, a census of the colony showed that of 21,000 inhabitants, 11,000 were slaves! This fact said much about the mentality that would dominate the economic development of the country.

In addition to this, the bulk of the European population was rural, living on isolated farms. They lived mostly according to strict patriarchal model, guided by a narrow interpretation of the Old Testament. These were the forging grounds of the Afrikaner mind, stubbornly prevailing against all opposition and reaching its extremity in the creation of apartheid in the twentieth century. This was also the beginning of the Afrikaner dialect, which became more and more distinct from Dutch, spoken by a colonial population that would soon find itself bereft of even a single real city.

The territorial expansion of this pseudo-colony was limited to a radius of sixty miles around Cape Town, extending mostly along the coastline, especially that bordering the Indian Ocean. When the settlers arrived there, the local population were mostly nomadic pastoralists whom the Dutch called "Hottentots." They were either expelled from the colonial lands, mostly into the desert of Karoo, or transformed into agricultural laborers.

Along the northeastern coast of the Indian Ocean an important border was established at the Great Fish River, separating the Cape colony from the Transkei lands of the Xhosas. Throughout the eighteenth century, this border was violated by armed skirmishes, raids, and reprisals. It was with the arrival of the English in 1815 that things came to a head, and destiny became more manifest.

The Boers, or Afrikaners,[15] felt that this was now their land, inherited from their ancestors who had arrived 150 years prior. They adamantly refused the right of these English foreigners to come and impose their own law. Their tremendous isolation, and their devotion to the Old Testament, had led them to consider themselves a new "chosen people," similar to the Israelites of the Bible. As late as 1948, the South African prime minister D.F. Malan declared, "In truth, the history of Afrikaners reveals a will and determination in which one can feel that *Afrikanerdom,* the Afrikaner community, is not the work of men, but of God."

When it became known in 1830 that the already detested English intended to abolish slavery, the situation became intolerable for the Afrikaners. In her popular memoirs, Anna Steenkamp wrote, "It is not the freeing of our slaves that angers us, it is having to watch them act as if they were the equals of Christian people. This is such a violation of both Divine Law and the natural differentiation of races and faiths, that no honest Christian can tolerate such a development." Nevertheless, Afrikaner life was fundamentally changed by the emancipation. Over 90 percent of Afrikaners were farmers, and they had to adapt to the transformation of their slaves into salaried workers. The entire economy and style of production was at stake.

Reacting with extraordinary, unyielding fanaticism, the Afrikaners decided to leave en masse. Beginning in 1837, they left the various areas of the Cape colony in great caravans of ox-drawn wagons, heading vaguely northwest. With a stubborn faith and great ignorance of Africa, some of them even believed that this "new Exodus"

---

[15] The term "Afrikaner" was apparently first used during a farmers' revolt against the Cape Town authorities in the mid-eighteenth century. See André Brink, *On the Contrary* (New York: Little, Brown & Co., 1994).

would lead them all the way to the Holy Land, the appropriate destination for a chosen people.

They were soon forced to detour northward around the mountains at the northwestern edge of the Transkei, which ended in Basutoland, now called Lesotho. The wagons of the Great Trek, as this adventure came to be known, succeeded in reaching far into the back country, through the *veldt*. One group of trekkers attempted to return back down toward the Natal coast, but the British, who had regarded their departure with amazement, now reacted vigorously. They seized control of the coastal province and drove the Afrikaners back northward.

Just to the east of the Transkei, in the Natal province, the Zulu King Chaka became the first African chieftain to adopt European principles of military organization. This began in 1820, and the Afrikaners of the Grand Trek were the first to feel the effects of it. It was only the superiority of their arms that saved them from destruction at the battle of Blood River on December 16, 1838.

The peace of the entire high veldt was already being disturbed by the Zulu expansion. It was further upset by the creation of the Transvaal Republic in the northwest, bordered by the Limpopo River (which certain trekkers believed to be the Red Sea), and by that of the Orange Free State, with Bloemfontein as its capital. These events also affected the Transkei, which had previously remained outside the currents of war. In fact, it was not until the end of the Boer War in 1902, only sixteen years before Rolihlahla's birth, that the situation became "normalized." Thus twentieth-century South African history was the painful outcome of this long and brutal conflict. Nelson Mandela would become a major participant in this history, yet he and his generation would follow a different course from that of their forefathers.

The repercussions of these troubles began to be felt heavily in the Transkei. To escape the Zulus, as well as the British, who finally annexed Natal in 1843, many coastal tribes began to migrate westward to the Transkei. This included the Mfengus, who arrived in

Xhosa territory in 1822, at the beginning of the troubles. This is relevant to our story because it was these people who came into conflict with the Thembus.

In 1825, the Mfengus defeated the Thembus near Hangklip. Then, in 1835, during the Border War, when the Xhosas were trying to prevent the whites from crossing the Kei River into the Transkei, 17,000 Mfengus crossed over to fight on the white side. This created such bitterness that Theophilus Shepstone, future Secretary for Native Affairs, began his career in 1838 with a major effort to make peace between the Xhosas and the Mfengus.

The Xhosa, and especially Thembu, acrimony is understandable. These so-called refugees from the east not only made war on their hosts, they joined the white enemy to the west, only to be shoved by their allies back into the Transkei among the Xhosas. These border wars only began to abate with the annexation of the Transkei. But the hatred would take much longer to dissolve. In 1925, two Mfengu descendants were living in the village of Qunu, the brothers George and Ben Mbekela. Most villagers shunned them, with an ancestral animosity based on memories of events almost a century prior.

Back in 1806, the Fish River had become the accepted border between the Transkei peoples' lands and those of the Cape colony. But the whites continued to push this border further eastward, from river to river: the Fish in 1806, the Keiska in 1824, the Kei in 1847, the Bashee (Rolihlahla's native land) in 1858, and the Mthatha in 1878. This finally culminated in the annexation of the Transkei in 1894.[16]

Nelson Mandela writes in his memoirs of the Mfengu descendants in Qunu, whom he remembers well. He maintains that his father did not share in the local prejudice against them. He also points out that the Mfengus were generally a socially advanced

---

[16] All these roughly parallel rivers begin in the mountains to the northwest and flow directly into the Indian Ocean (see map on page 143).

group. (George Mbekela was a retired teacher, and his brother was a policeman.) Of course, this can be explained by their ancestral alliance, and the consequent European influence. But it was, in fact, George who advised Nosekeni to send Rolihlahla to school. This man had a great influence on her. He was a devout Christian and also convinced her to convert. Her Christian name was Fanny. This also led to Rolihlahla being baptized in the Methodist Church.

School was a far more significant event for the boy. No one in his family had ever attended before, and Nosekeni had to consult with her husband about it. Without hesitation, he enrolled Rolihlahla in the Qunu primary school.

On his first day, he had to abandon the traditional clothing he had worn exclusively up to date: a long cloth attached at the shoulder and wrapped around the waist. He exchanged this for an old pair of pants that had belonged to his father. The legs had to be cut shorter, and a length of cord tied at the waist to hold them up. "I have never been prouder in my life," he recalls.

The schoolhouse was a rectangular brick building with a corrugated metal roof. On the first day, the teacher gave him an English first name which would stick: Nelson. This was the first step in a process of acculturation. The British, like other European colonial powers of those days, could barely conceive of such a thing as "African culture." One of the avowed purposes of colonialism was to "civilize the savages." The two pillars of this ideology were the Christian church and the school. So it was that Rolihlahla Madiba Mandela, who had already been baptized as a Christian, now became Nelson Mandela. With the influence of years of elementary school, high school, and university, he would progressively absorb "a British education, British ideas, and British culture."

And of course this meant learning English. At the age of six, he spoke only Xhosa, like his parents. His father knew only a smattering of English from his interactions with local white administrators. For the boy (named Nelson by the teacher, after an Admiral of whom he knew nothing), learning to read and write also meant learning to speak English for the first time. Yet Xhosa, like other African languages, was well-established as a written language in those days. The first Xhosa newspaper, *Ikwezi*, "The Morning Star," had been published as far back as 1841. The first Xhosa translations of the Gospels dated from 1854, and the entire Bible appeared in that language in 1883.[17]

This imposition of the English language upon a different culture had its advantages. It had the effect of opening doors for educated Africans into the dominant European culture, and into modern South African society. It was certainly thanks partly to his youthful mastery of English that Nelson Mandela would be able to realize his destiny as lawyer, leader of the ANC, and ultimately president of the country. Later on, he would make good use of his prison years in learning Afrikaans, the language of the enemy. But for him, the undertaking was one of trying to *understand* his enemies by learning their language, and thereby their culture and ways of thinking.

Yet it was not upward social mobility through education that the whites, especially those in the government, had in mind. They especially wanted to train native African administrators to run their reservations for them. Such men would have to be bilingual, so as to communicate governmental orders to the local populations.

If they had allowed classes to be conducted in Xhosa, this would have been a double-edged sword for the Africans. On the one hand, it would enable them to affirm a cultural and even national identity, and allow children like Nelson to develop their culture without forsaking its roots. But this would also close children like him into a linguistic and cultural ghetto. As a matter of fact, the apartheid government belatedly realized this in 1961, when they began to mount an assault on English, requiring that the black

---

[17] It was also during this period that the first newspaper in the Afrikaans language appeared, *Die Patriot.*

university at Fort Hare, which Mandela had attended in 1940, conduct its classes only in native African languages.

Thus his new world of education and language, so different from that of his parents and ancestors, was to become more and more his home. The gulf between the two worlds could only grow greater as the years passed.

Yet because he came from the heart of the Transkei, the heart of an Africa which had been relatively protected from the most intense British and Afrikaner interference, he was also able to receive a traditional African upbringing outside of school. Through his play, extracurricular activities, and daily life, and through listening to stories of the elders, he would remain profoundly African. This dual education is important in understanding his militant convictions in the 1950s, his dignity as political prisoner from the 1960s through the 1980s, and his extraordinary statesmanship in the 1990s.

Pastoral Childhood

"Boys were practically left to themselves," says Nelson Mandela in writing about his childhood.

Boys were the customary guardians of the livestock herds. But since the vast pastures now had fences to keep the animals from roaming indefinitely, they had leisure to do almost as they pleased. "Nature was our playground," he adds. The games they played resembled games of children around the world, especially in rural areas.

Besides the European games passed on by those who attended school, there were many of their own traditional games. Some of them were simply playful systems for deciding who had do a chore, such as finding a strayed cow or gathering a scattered herd back together. One of these games is called *Ingcaka*. Two boys stand facing each other, arms outstretched toward each other with closed fists. One of them is dubbed *u-Hlanga* (from the verb "to meet"), and the other *i-Mpamba* (from the verb "to cross"). The two players then extend the fingers of one hand, each at the same instant. If the two hands are both right hands, or both left hands, then two points are won by *i-Mpamba*. If there is one right hand and one left hand, two points are won by *u-Hlanga*. Hence there are only even numbers scored, and the loser after ten (or sometimes twenty) points has to go do the chore.

Another game resembles our drawing straws. Several grass stems are gathered in a bundle, one of which has a ribbon of grass leaf tied around it. One boy presents the bundle to the others, so that

the ribbon is concealed. Whoever draws the stem with the ribbon
has to go look for the lost cow.

The system of scoring points with right and left hands is also
used in other games. It is not unlike the American children's game
of "rock-paper-scissors." In a game called "Horse Race," for example, this system replaces dice. A racetrack is drawn in the dirt as
shown in the following figure.

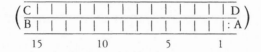

The race begins at A, usually with two players. Two pebbles or
grains of corn are placed there, representing the horses. The two
players face off at each end of the racetrack, and play the game
of *Ingcaka* as described above. The winner of each point moves his
horse along the lines, rather than in the squares. The first to arrive
at D wins. Transkei boys love this game and play it for hours when
the weather is not too warm.

When it rains or the sun is too hot, other games are played under
shelter. In one of these, the fleshy stems of a plant resembling
rhubarb are used. They are cut into pieces about two to three inches
long, until there is a large pile of them on the ground. Then each
boy in turn attempts to spear and retrieve as many of them as possible. He uses a short stick of wood, which has been whittled to a
sharp point at one end, twisting it sharply between thumb and fore-
finger in a single movement, which is all he is allowed on his turn.
Rolihlahla was adept at this game, and sometimes would spear three
or four pieces at once. But on other turns he might fail to retrieve
any. The game is over when the pile is gone, and the winner is the
one who has speared and retrieved the most stems.

Qobongo is a game of memory played mostly indoors, which is
typical of small peasant societies such as this. Each person tries to

recall the names of as many birds as possible. Two boys face off, placing pebbles or kernels of corn between them, which are used as counters. The first player gives a grain of corn to the other, and then chants: "*Qobonbo ntaka-ni le?*" (*Qobonbo, what bird is it?*) The other must then answer with no hesitation allowed, "It's a partridge," or "It's a heron," etc. The players continue like this, always chanting or singing their dialogue, until the bird-namer hesitates. Then he must give the grains to his adversary and challenge him to name birds in turn. The other children are grouped around and accompany the musical dialogue with their own humming.

Some children are able to recite as many as thirty or forty names of birds; and there are a great multitude to be found in their land—the *hadeda*, with its ominous cry and silhouette, the white heron perched on the backs of the cows, the white-breasted crow, the swan, the red-winged thrush, the *concal* which sings before it rains, the various hawks and vultures, the sociable weaverbird, which lives in colonies, sewing dozens of nests onto a single tree branch, and the black widow, a tiny bird with a tail so long that one wonders how it can possibly fly.

Girls have their own special games. The simplest, usually for very young girls, is called *ngomso mkozi* (*mkozi* is a term of courtesy in refined society). Ten or twelve girls form a line, one behind the other, with hands on the shoulders of the girl in front. All close their eyes, except for the first in line, who is the leader. They walk, singing the refrain *Siya kufika ninina?* ("When are we going to arrive?") Finally the leader answers: *Sifikile!* ("We've arrived!") Everyone opens their eyes to see where they are, and they all scatter, laughing.

One common activity of girls is making beaded jewelry: necklaces, bracelets for wrist, arm, knee, and ankle, headbands, and belts. Sometimes they offer such jewelry to boys.

In traditional ceremonies, similar beadwork is worn by adults as well, sometimes including very elaborate patterns sewn in a vest or apron. Historically, such beadwork, inlaid with copper wire, was a major item of trade with whites. The colors of the beads are usually pale: sky-blue, white, pink, yellow, etc. Red is reserved for chiefs. Beadwork jewelry is an indispensable element of all important celebrations: marriage engagements, weddings, dances, and religious ceremonies.

In Johannesburg in the 1950s, Nelson Mandela had himself photographed in traditional Xhosa dress, with a necklace made of over a dozen rows of beads of different colors. (See photo, page 133.) This open affirmation of his African roots was deeply significant, for it took place during a period before it became fashionable to do so, and when he was already working as a lawyer and political activist in that city.

During his trial in 1962, Winnie Mandela (also a Xhosa) sat in the first row of the public, wearing different traditional Xhosa dresses each day, adorned with the typical bead necklaces.

From his later childhood, Mandela remembers a special game which boys could require girls to play when they wished to be associate with them. It was called *Khetha,* which signifies "choose the one you like." Each girl would choose a boy, who then had the right to accompany her the rest of the way home or wherever. "But the girls were sharper than the boys," he recalls. Sometimes they would deliberately choose a boy only because they felt like making fun of him. He confesses it was his favorite game to play with girls, but does not reveal whether this ever happened to him.

But in general, the boys preferred to play by themselves. Rolihlahla, nicknamed Buti by his sisters, ran wild over the hills and meadows with his pals. They would catch birds, eat eggs from their nests, weave themselves necklaces of little shells, and swim in the river when it was hot. This was the occasion for a game where one boy would swim underwater and try to touch another boy, who would do his best to escape. When he was touched, he had to swim underwater and catch another boy in his turn.

After this they would lie around on the riverbank. Often, like children all over southern Africa, they would use clay to sculpt little animals, which they would dry in the sun—cows, pigs, horses, and others. They would also make little wagons out of twigs, hitched to their clay oxen. Each boy would gradually build up a kind of miniature farm of his own and spend hours playing with it.

Sometimes they would just lounge after swimming, doing nothing. In his novel, *A Chain of Voices,* André Brink describes South African children, both black and white, after a swim:

> When tired of playing and swimming, they would often lie on the grass, almost naked, chewing on stems of grass or herbs. Sometimes they would stare together at the clouds, to see who could describe the most inventive forms in them: a cow with an enormous udder, a pair of oxen, a wagon, a face, a closed fist, a sock, a woman's breasts, a heron ...
>
> Sometimes they would lie there so long they would forget about their work— birds might be raiding the crops [...] and there were vegetables to be picked, cows to be milked, and wood to be chopped.

One of the most popular games was *u-tinti,* meaning "throw the lance." This was a game to develop warrior's skills. Rolihlahla was one of the very top lancers. The boys split into two teams, each of which planted a sharpened wooden stick, or lance, in the ground about thirty yards apart. Then one team member would take his lance and throw it toward the lance of the other team. If he touched it, he cried *Inti!* and went to get his stick back. If he succeeded in making it fall, he was allowed to throw all his remaining sticks beyond those of the opposing team, and then a whole process of retrieving them was played through. After this, the game started all over again.

In his autobiography, Mandela says this was an "imitation of war." The game was so popular that even when they were older, Nelson and his friends organized matches against the boys of neighboring villages. He adds that "those who distinguished themselves in these matches were greatly admired, as if they were generals who had achieved military victories."

The boys carried their wooden sticks with them everywhere. They served both as useful tools (for goading the cattle, for example) and as toys for their games. Another of these games was *i-ngqolodi,* whose object was throw a lance which had a real spear tip on it, in such a fashion that it would not stick in the ground but would bounce up and flip over and over like the spokes of a wheel. The boy whose spear flipped over the most times won.

It is obvious that such games, especially *u-tinti,* developed combat skills in the boys. Sometimes this would degenerate into fights. An example of this was called *um-ngeni,* "the battle of the boys," which actually involved adolescents who had not yet undergone the circumcision rite of initiation into adulthood. Some banal quarrel (sometimes within the tribe, sometimes involving youths of a different tribe) could be the spark which set off a battle between different groups. Those who felt offended could only regain their honor in combat. Insults would be exchanged and a date set for battle.

One of the groups walked to the edge of their territory and sat waiting. When the other group arrived, they would exchange more mockery and insults, heating themselves up.

Girls accompanied each group, yelling to excite the boys if their courage appeared to waver. They screamed and clapped their hands, accusing the slackers of cowardice.

Each combatant had several sticks, which could be serious weapons. One stick was knotted, and another was a longer and smoother lance with a sharpened end. There was also a short club with a rounded end. The latter was the most dangerous weapon. It was used in close fighting to knock down an opponent, but it could also be hurled at someone out of reach. A kind of blanket was used to protect the arm holding the weapon.

Some of these battles could turn very ugly, especially if adults became involved. This sometimes resulted in serious wounds and even deaths. Then a thirst for vengeance could lead to reprisals and more fighting. But the boys' battle scars were worn with great pride.

Combat with sticks

In his memoirs, Mandela writes, "I learned to fight with a stick—
an indispensable skill for African country boys—and became adept
in the various fighting techniques: parrying blows, feinting in one
direction and striking in another, and fast legwork to escape an
adversary's attack." He says no more, yet it is clear that he does not
regard these fights as mere sport. Years later, at Fort Hare University, he learned boxing. The language he used in speaking of
this martial art was exactly like that he used in speaking of the stick
fighting. This is another example of the confluence of two worlds
in him: the African and the British.

But most of the boys' games were more peaceful, such as *um-tshot-
sho,* a musical game. It is remarkable in that it is not exactly singing
or dancing, though it has elements of both. One missionary wrote:

> One might describe it as a series of sounds of a barbaric
> music, covering an entire musical octave. The singers emit
> tones, not in the natural manner of singing, but with an arti-
> ficial usage of the larynx and epiglottis. Once the ear
> becomes accustomed to it, one may experience great pleas-
> ure in hearing boys chant their *um-tshotsho.* But for the unini-
> tiated ear, it appears strange, wild, and barbaric.[18]

Nature was more than just a playground for the boys. The same
missionary, a man of mixed African and European blood, continues:

> The immense *veldt* is the native children's classroom. Its mys-
> teries are already opening before them, while their Euro-
> pean counterparts are still in kindergarten. Because they
> have the task of tending to the goats, sheep, horses, and cat-
> tle, they learn everything about these animals at a very young
> age: their behavior, their peculiarities, their coloring, their
> reproductive habits, and the ways that different species rest,

---

[18] John Henderson Soga, *The Ama-Xhosa: Life and Customs* (Johannesburg:
Alice Lovedale Press, 1931).

sleep, and wake up. A native child can tell you in exactly what manner animals with horns, as compared to horses, bend their fore or hind legs when lying down, and how they get up again. Few civilized children have this kind of knowledge.

Writing sixty years later than this missionary, Nelson Mandela seems to echo his feelings when he recalls that "This was the beginning of my love for the *veldt*, for the great open spaces, the simple beauty of nature, and the pure line of the horizon."

A Terminal Cough

In 1927, when Rolihlahla was nine years old, his father came unexpectedly into his mother's hut in the middle of the night. The boy was awed at the ensuing consternation in the kraal, for his father was lying on the floor, seized by a fit of coughing which seemed interminable. In fact, he was already in the terminal stages of tuberculosis which had never been treated. He would live on for another week, nursed by Nosekeni and by his youngest wife. In his last moments, he asked to smoke his pipe, and died before it had gone out.

It was a rude shock for the young boy. Although his mother was the center of his life, his father had been a towering image of strength and dignity, all the more impressive for his long absences. But, of course, his pain and bewilderment were essentially like that of any child whose father has died.

For the Xhosas, death is not an extinction. For Rolihlahla, this attitude was further reinforced by his mother's Methodist influence. Both Christianity and traditional African beliefs agreed that the soul or spirit of the deceased continues to live on in another realm which is vague, but real. For the Xhosas, the dead also communicate with the living. In spite of this and other differences, the realm of the ancestors would appear to have important resemblances to the heaven of the Christians; and the often naive images employed by the missionaries only encouraged this comparison.

For the Xhosas, even animals continue to live on in the afterworld. Like his friends, young Rolihlahla believed that this was a land of hills and valleys, running streams and forests. And it had cows, sheep, goats, and horses grazing in its fields—a kind of replica of the Transkei, in effect. Yet everything was spiritualized there. There was no need to labor and harvest crops in that realm. One word was enough to materialize your every desire. When you married, you didn't have to build your house. It was a kind of Eden, or paradise.

The mystery of death was feared more than death itself. The departed were mourned for a limited period. Its purpose was both to express one's own pain, and to announce the event—to one's neighbors and to the ancestral spirits.

As soon as their husband was dead, Nosekeni and his other wife folded his arms across his chest and placed his hands on his shoulders. Then they bent his legs at the knees and forced them up upon his chest, holding all four members in this position until the corpse began to stiffen there. Without having either his eyes or his mouth closed, he was now in the appropriate posture for burial.

Some men dug a shallow grave, less than four feet deep, and barely three feet wide. The body, with folded arms and legs, was placed there in an upright sitting position, with plenty of room to spare. Just before the body of their beloved was dropped, Nosekeni and Rolihlahla tossed his personal affairs into the bottom of the grave—his clothes, his sleeping mat, his wooden pillow, his goatskin sack, and his pipe. A small hollow had been dug at the bottom and against the side of the grave, and it was here that Henry Gadla's body came to rest, on top of his clothes, wrapped in a shroud. Following tradition, his face was turned toward his house, since he had died of an illness. This would help the spirit of the departed to watch over his family and keep away ill fortune. Since Rolihlahla's father had been a chief, he was buried to the left of the entrance to his kraal.

Then the men filled the grave, packing the dirt with layers of rocks and thorny branches to keep animals, especially dogs, from digging there. The men who had carried the body and dug the grave then went to purify themselves by ritually washing in a stream.

These rituals of farewell to the mortal remains of Henry Gadla Mphakanyiswa were imbued with love, respect, and grief. As in all human societies, such rituals helped the bereaved to at least accept death, if not to understand it.

The following day, Nosekeni shaved Rolihlahla's head. His mourning period would last until his hair grew back.

But his father's death was to have other consequences. A few days later, Nosekeni explained to her son that he must now leave Qunu to go live at the court of the sovereign chief of the Thembus, Jongintaba Daweti, who would be his guardian. But this title "sovereign chief," invented by colonial authorities, lacks precision. The term "king," or "regent," might be a more accurate translation of his traditional role.

Jongintaba was the second son of King Kalindyebo, who died in 1920, followed by his eldest son, Jongilizwe in 1926. Jongilizwe's own son, the prince Sabata, was too young to rule, and Jongintaba was named Regent. The invitation to young Rolihlahla to come live with him was a sort of adoption, even though he already had a son of his own. As son of a chief, Rolihlahla was expected to be a companion to this son of a king (or regent), Justice Bambilanga. They would spend much time together throughout the years leading up to their initiation ceremonies, which they would also undergo together.

Not long before his death, Henry Gadla Mphakanyiswa had presented Rolihlahla to Jongintaba. This was partly out of respect for custom, but also because he sensed that his days were numbered. This explains why Nosekeni's decision to let her son go was not abnormal. She had known for some time that her husband was seriously ill. Though she was illiterate, it was she who had convinced him to send Rolihlahla to school. Of course this was at the urging of George Mbekela, but it was also because she had understood, through her contacts with Methodist pastors, that the whole of the Transkei and South Africa was undergoing great upheaval.

In all the villages, young men were now leaving to work in the gold mines of Johannesburg. They would rarely, if ever, return to live in their villages. They would send a part of their salaries to their families. This would cease when a young man got married there, often outside of his ancestral tradition. If he was to pay the *lobola,* or dowry, to the girl's parents, it was no longer in livestock as in his parents' time, but in money. None of those who lived in the city could afford to be polygamous.

When Nosekeni decided to entrust Rolihlahla to the sovereign chief, it was out of selfless love for him and intelligent concern for his future. He would continue his studies, which would make him better adapted to the modern world. Living at the Regent's court would provide a protection for this, at least until his stay reached its term according to custom.

It was early morning when she and her son left Qunu for the six-mile walk across the fields to Mqekezweni, the Regent's village. Rolihlahla wore his short pants, made from his father's old khaki trousers, and a shirt of the same color. He had packed all his belongings in a little metal suitcase. Even sixty years later, he remembers this departure with great emotion: "Qunu was all I had ever known, and I loved it with that boundless love that children have for their home."

Until then, his universe had been bordered by the familiar hills that reached to the horizon. In this magical space of childhood, he knew every human face, every meadow, and tree. Beyond this lay the apprehension of the unknown.

But life continued at Qunu without him, until a day, many years later, when he returned to the village to see it for the last time, before it disappeared forever as he knew it. He writes that he looked from a distance upon the three round huts where he had known the love and protection of his mother. And just after he turned away from them for the last time, as he believed, he was filled with a poignant regret—he wished he had gone and embraced the huts before leaving.

Mqekezweni is located on a small road which today is the link between National Highway 2 and the road between Umtata and Engcobo. It was still an unpaved road when I took it one summer morning in January 1990, in a pounding rain. I almost missed the turn onto a little stone bridge built over a shallow stream running six feet below. The car's tires passed only an inch or so from the unprotected edge, risking an inglorious end to our expedition!

Three boys about ten years old watched us slide along the wet, slippery little road, their heads covered by plastic bags to keep the rain off. In the distance, there were some mimosa trees. For an instant, I was reminded of Nelson Mandela and his pals sixty years earlier, sitting on a hillside, telling each other stories. Apparently there had been little change in this landscape of hills, water, and sky.

The children remained still as we pulled up next to them. They confirmed that the next village was indeed Mqekezweni. We had rented the car at Umtata, but the license plates were from Johannesburg. They were probably wondering what on earth these whites, probably Afrikaners, were doing in this remote area. Had they any idea that Nelson Mandela, still in prison on that January day in 1990, had spent his own childhood there?

As we climbed the last rise to the village, we finally saw another vehicle going the other way, an ancient Ford pickup.

Mqekezweni resembles all villages in that area. It is doubtful that Rolihlahla found it a strange place when he arrived here after three hours of walking through the pastures. Over half a century later, there are still round straw huts with conical thatched roofs. There are also some slightly larger rectangular brick houses with corrugated tin roofs. And a building with Gothic windows, which is apparently the church.

I imagine nine-year-old Rolihlahla arriving here, walking with his mother among the round huts, carrying his little suitcase. The other children must have wondered what was inside it as they stood staring with curiosity. It was Makhulu, the sovereign chief's wife, who welcomed Nosekeni and her son in front of the "Big House," a round hut with thatched roof like the others, but much larger. The walls were whitened with chalk. Mandela remembers his impression of this as a beautiful and spacious house. It even had a wooden floor inside, which was the height of luxury to this child from Qunu.

The whole of the Regent's kraal consisted of seven round huts and two rectangular houses. Makhulu led Rolihlahla to a hut about ten yards behind the main house. He would share this with Justice, and the two young boys would soon become like brothers. Inside there were two beds, a table, and an oil lamp.

While he was taking in this new environment which was to be his, an automobile, a Ford V8, arrived in a cloud of dust and came to a stop. A not very tall man, dressed in a European suit, got out. A group of men who had been sitting in the shade all got up and cried, "Greetings, Jongintaba!" Rolihlahla stood rooted to his spot, watching the sovereign chief greet the men, who were members of his council. This Ford was an impressive sign of his power.

Now he understood that a different life was beginning for him. He took his mother's hand and hugged close against her. Yet at the same time he was fascinated by these signs of wealth and authority. "It was at this moment," he writes, "that I realized that life had more to offer me than just being a champion stick-fighter."

But his life among the children of Mqekezweni was not very different from that of Qunu. There were the same games, the same running through the fields, the same ears of corn that they would steal from a garden, roast on a little fire they built far from the huts, and eat with delight. One day Rolihlahla was caught stealing an ear of corn from the garden of the pastor, Maryolo. Sixty years later, he vividly recalled the sting of remorse for this transgression, and the pain of his punishment as well.

Later, when he was more integrated into his new life, Jongintaba would—rarely—allow him to indulge in one of his greatest delights: galloping through the hills on a horse.

Justice was four years older than Rolihlahla, and already in middle school. Nelson attended elementary school at Mqekezweni. He had three teachers: Zama Njozela, Arthur Geikwe, and Mabel Mtirara (the latter belonged to another branch of the royal family). The children were divided into two levels of classes. They studied English, Xhosa, math, geography, and history—British history.

On several occasions, including his memoirs, Nelson Mandela has claimed that he had no special talent, and had to work hard to succeed in his studies. It is true that during his entire life, beginning in childhood, others considered him a "serious" individual. Yet when one takes his whole career into account, including his university studies, his law diploma, his responsibilities as head of the ANC, and his extraordinary political insight, it is hard to believe that he was just a hard-working student with average abilities.

After classes, the boys would go play in the fields. They also had chores to do, like country children everywhere. They had to milk the cows, who stayed outside. Sometimes they would drink warm milk directly from the cow. Then they brought the full buckets back to the kraal.

Jongintaba and his first wife, Noh-England,[19] were strict, but they raised Nelson with kindness, as if he were one of their own children. The boy's seriousness earned him the nickname "Grandfather." The two dominant influences in village life were the chief's court and the church. In Qunu, he had only gone to church to be baptized, but in Mqekezweni he never missed the sermon or Sunday school. This was because of the chief's piety, but also because of the personality of Reverend Maryolo, a warm and friendly man who commanded respect.

Nelson was well-qualified to form an opinion of the chief's court, since he essentially lived there. What he saw and learned from this would have a decisive influence in his later life. The sometimes novel perspectives which he would offer during the negotiations

---

[19] This name means "Mother-England."

between 1990 and 1994, especially his systematic quest for consensus, were in large part due to this training at the chief's court. In his autobiography, he writes: "The concept I would later form of what it means to give an order was profoundly influenced by the spectacle of the king and his court."

Among the Xhosas, the chief's word has the force of law, but only because he has to respect tribal customs and live according to them. He would never dare make certain decisions or actions which are in violation of these customs. Thus before taking any action, he reflects upon how it will be judged by members of the tribe.

Whenever there was an important problem to be resolved, Jongintaba sent a letter to all the Thembu chiefs, summoning them to court. The chiefs then gathered at Mqekezweni, and the Regent welcomed them and listened to them. They spoke freely, and there were frequent, sometimes caustic criticisms, of which he was often the target. He accepted these without emotion. No decision was taken until a consensus was reached. This process could take a long time, because the consensus had to be complete. It was never acceptable for a majority to impose its will upon a minority of dissenters.

"In my roles as leader, I have always followed the principles which I saw the King apply in the Big House," Nelson Mandela later wrote. This was true during the years when he was head of the ANC, mostly in the 1950s. And it is perhaps even truer of the years after he left prison in 1990 to become president. Nelson Mandela refused to content himself with the easy path of majority rule when he had to deal with the whole array of mutually hostile forces of South Africa's recent history: the National Party (the Afrikaner whites who invented apartheid); the Afrikaner Front, a party of white extremists led by General Viljoen,[20] former head of the South African armed forces; the Inkatha, a Zulu party led by Chief Gatsha Butelezi, who had formed an alliance with the Afrikaner National Party; and

---

[20] This name actually comes from the French name Villon.

the Pan-African Congress, a black party of the extreme left, born from a split in the ANC during the 1950s.

To settle for a majority decision which marginalized these important minorities would be a sell-out of his vision for the future: nothing less than the reconstruction of a new South Africa. Any political group, or leader of an important community, who was cast out of the political process, could become a time bomb that might later set off the civil war the vast majority dreaded, and a few hoped for. In applying these principles of consensus, Nelson Mandela not only became a political teacher for South Africa, but for the Western world as well. At the time of this writing, in the late 1990s, this consensus process has so far triumphed over all obstacles, even though the National Party left the governmental coalition, and even though Frederik de Klerk resigned his post as second vice-president of the Republic. Nor has the hegemony of the ANC been shaken by the efforts of a new party, created by General Viljoen in alliance with the Bantu General Holomiza, former prime minister of the Transkei during apartheid. Whatever the future may have in store for South Africa, we can say today that it is thanks to Nelson Mandela, and to the indigenous African democratic traditions that he learned in childhood, that this historic first step in South Africa's transformation has been such a success.

Rolihlahla would also discover an entirely different history at the court of the Thembu king. It was the oral history of the peoples of South Africa, especially the Thembus and other Xhosas of the Transkei. At school, the only history which seemed to exist was that of Great Britain and Europe. As for South Africa, its history began on April 7, 1652, with the arrival of Europeans at the Cape of Good Hope: Jan van Riebeeck and the ninety employees of the Dutch East India Company.

When the debates of Jongintaba's council of chiefs finally came to an end, the elders would sit in a circle and tell stories of the greatness of days past. Rolihlahla would draw close to listen to them. At first he was chased away because he was too young. But he persisted, and they finally got used to him, and allowed him to listen. He would sit at the edge of the circle of light from the fire burning in the night, listening avidly to tales of past heroes and their deeds.

Among these chiefs was a very old man who was the main keeper of the collective memory of the Thembus. His name was Joyi Zwelibhangile; he was a son of the great chief Ngubengcuka, who had ruled from 1809 to 1832, as well as the brother of King Mtirara. Rolihlahla considered him as a sort of great-great-uncle. "He was so old," wrote Nelson Mandela, "that his wrinkled skin hung on him like a loose-fitting coat."

Among the stories he told was that of Chaka and the Zulu people. This was the story of Makana, a Xhosa chief who, in 1819, attacked the city of Grahamstown, leading an army of 10,000 men. The glory of such African warriors excited young Rolihlahla's imagination. And the memories of the tales he heard in his childhood would always remain with him. One might even say that it is in those memories that he finds his deepest roots, and his human dignity. His pride in his own African heritage would later become the source of his legitimacy as a political activist. This was manifest in his struggles as leader of the ANC, in his leadership of the armed, clandestine group, Umkhonto we Sizwe, as well as in his years of arduous work in his prison cell at Robben Island.

At his trial in 1962, he told his judges:

> Many years ago, when I was a child in my village in the Transkei, I would listen to the tribal elders who told stories of the good old days before the white man came.... This country belongs to us.... The elders recounted the history of the wars in which our ancestors fought to defend our country, and the bravery of our officers and soldiers in those epic times.

At the famous Rivonia trial in 1964, when he was sentenced to life imprisonment, he spoke again on this subject:

In my youth in the Transkei, I listened to the elders of my tribe recount our history. Some of these were accounts of the wars fought by our ancestors to defend their country. The illustrious names of Dingane, Bambatha, Hintsa, Makana, Dalasile, Moshoeshoe, and Sekhukhune[21] were revered as the glory of all the African nations. It is my hope that life will give me the opportunity to serve my people and to add my humble contribution to this struggle of liberation. *This is the motivating force behind all of my acts,*[22] and behind all of the accusations brought against me during this trial.

Thus Rolihlahla, only a boy of twelve, listened eagerly in the tiny village of Mqekezweni to Joyi's stories of the great deeds of the past. Thirty years later, as Nelson Mandela, he would add his own revolutionary actions to this long record of the African chiefs' struggles against white tyranny.

---

[21] Here, Mandela is citing names of chiefs from all the major tribes and regions of South Africa. Dingane was a Zulu chief who died in 1840. He was the half-brother of Chaka. Bambatha, also a Zulu chief, was his contemporary. Hintsa was a Xhosa chief who died in 1820. Dalasile, another Xhosa chief, was the son of Kreli, who died in 1863. Moshoeshoe was a Sotho chief who lived from 1786 to 1870.

[22] These are the author's italics.

An Excess of Prophets

Chief Joyi Zwelibhangile's heroic stories had their dark and desolate moments also. At such times he would put away the sword which he had drawn, standing, in dramatic illustration of his narrative, and sit down quietly. The fire would be stoked with more wood, and he would continue in a more somber tone. Even though the Transkei had been relatively protected by the mountains from the major currents of war which ravaged the high veldt in the nineteenth century, the peoples who lived there had still suffered greatly. This was especially true of the Xhosas.

Their warrior's heroism could not prevail indefinitely. Faced with military defeats, the loss of lands, the treachery of tribes who joined with the whites, the growth of Christian churches and schools, and with powerful forces which threatened the very existence and identity of traditional peoples and ancestral ways of life, people's reactions soon changed from anger to despair.

As their forces were shown to be insufficient, and their arms to be ineffectual against those of the enemy, they turned more and more to the spirits of the ancestors for help and guidance.

Prophets abounded. They all advocated various rituals of purification, which were followed for the most part. Their influence was on the rise as early as 1819, when Makana attacked Grahamstown, a white city located between the Ciskei and the Transkei. He was neither a king nor a high chieftain, but an *i-tola*, a kind of warrior-priest and soothsayer. After being captured in 1820, he drowned while escaping from Robben Island. The Xhosas, who believed he had supernatural powers, would wait a long time before abandoning hope for his return.

Some twenty years afterward, a young Xhosa named Mlanjeni became famous for his denunciation of sorcerers, and his exhortation of the different tribes to purify themselves of all sorcery. He gained the support of the Sotho chief Moshoeshoe, and of the Mpondo chief Faku. Somehow he managed to convince everyone that he, too, was an *i-tola*, and that he had the power to immobilize the enemy. He ordered the slaughter of all dark-colored cattle. He promised victory to the Xhosas by changing the whites' rifles into water. In order to accomplish this, he insisted they offer sacrifices to the ancestral spirits and abandon all sorcery. But it was his promises which turned to water in the disastrous war against the whites that broke out in 1851.

Rolihlahla listened with a lump in his throat to the narrative of his ancestors' defeats, which only increased their despair and made them turn even more toward their traditional religious beliefs.

Beginning in 1854, the Xhosas began to hear talk in mission schools of the Crimean War. Somehow they got the notion that the Russians were also blacks who were fighting against the English enemy. A rumor spread that the English were dying of cholera, and that the Russians would soon defeat them and come to Africa to help the Xhosas push them back to the sea.

Then, in March of 1856, a young girl named Nongqause told her uncle Mhlakaza, an advisor to the Xhosa chief Sarili, that she had seen "men with strange cattle" coming out of the river where she went to get water. Mhlakaza went to see for himself, and also saw the strange men. They told him to return to his kraal, and to undergo three days of purification. Then, on the fourth day, he was to sacrifice a cow and return on the following day to meet them again. Mhlakaza obeyed, thus launching the strangest and most tragic catastrophe of modern Xhosa history. Its scars and repercussions would be felt right down to the time of Nelson Mandela himself.

When Mhlakaza returned to the riverbank five days later, he saw a great number of black men, among whom he recognized his brother, who had died several years before. These men told him that they came from the other side of the water, and that they were the "Russians" who had been waging constant war against the English. They had come to help the Xhosas, under the condition that they abandon all sorcery. Furthermore, they must slaughter all their livestock. They would not be needing it, since abundant herds would be given to them after the day of resurrection.[23]

Now the visions began to multiply. Young Nongqause saw "the horns of magnificent cows among the reeds." Chief Sarili himself saw one of his horses who had died long ago. The message coming from both the ancestral spirits and the "Russians" was always the same: purification; abandonment of sorcery; and sacrifices. Nongqause proclaimed that the Xhosas must sacrifice all their reserves of grain, as well as all their livestock. When this was done, and the Xhosas had nothing left to eat, the heroes of yesteryear would all return, and everyone alive would be young. The huts would all be full of grain, and the most beautiful English cattle would appear in their corrals. Huge numbers of wagons would appear, filled with clothes, rifles, and ammunition. A great wind would rise, and the whites would be pushed back into the sea.

In spite of some people's misgivings, this paroxysm could not be stopped, and the Xhosas prepared to engage in a suicidal enterprise. The efforts of Charles Brownlee, the English administrator, to stop the insanity only reinforced the convictions of the Xhosa believers.

In October, 1856, Nongqause proclaimed that all the animals must be killed within a week and that the dead would return on the eighth day. Of course nothing happened on the eighth day, but the believers blamed those who had hesitated and held back hoards of livestock and grain. Nongqause then announced that on February 18,

---

[23] According to official report of the administrator, Charles Brownlee.

1857, two red suns would appear in the sky, a great wind would rise, and the spirits of the ancestors would destroy both the English and those Xhosas who refused to believe her prophecies.

During the following months, the Xhosas slaughtered an estimated 150,000 to 200,000 cattle, and virtually all their livestock. On February 18, 1857, no red suns dawned, and no ancestors arrived to chase the English away.

Famine ravaged the country. The missions distributed some food, but it was far from enough. The new hospital at King William's Town was full of people dying of starvation. The bishops of Grahamstown and Cape Town organized the Kafir[24] Assistance Society. Thousands of Xhosa families were forced to migrate to Cape Province and work on white farms.

Charles Brownlee estimated that 20,000 died, and that another 30,000 left the Transkei. According to some witnesses, Nongqause survived, and was still working as a servant on a white farm in Alexandria in 1905. But John Henderson Soga claims that she died at King William's Town in 1897.

Many questions have been asked in an effort to understand the causes of this terrible "cattle killing," as it has come to be called. Some have theorized that it was a cunning, despotic manipulation concocted by Chief Sarili: when the Xhosas were hungry and had nothing left to lose, the chiefs would become filled with the spirits of the ancestral heroes, and the people would have no choice but to ferociously attack in a grand offensive against the Cape colony. Proponents of this theory point out that horses, which are essential to war, were not included in the orders to slaughter, supposedly communicated by the ancestors through the voice of

---

[24] *Kafir* is a word of Arabic origin, meaning "non-believer." It was often applied to non-Muslim peoples in eastern and southern Africa, but it was originally neither a racist nor a pejorative term. Dutch colonists borrowed this word, and it became a term of disdain for all indigenous peoples in southern Africa. Today, it has become approximately as inflammatory as the English word "nigger," and is generally taboo.

Nongqause. Furthermore, the whole undertaking was never debated in Sarili's chief's council, which goes against tradition.

Others have argued that if any manipulation took place, it was the whites, and in particular the missionaries, who must have been behind it. Its objective would be to destroy Xhosa power once and for all, so as to easily annex the Transkei.

But these are only speculations. Some historians have pointed out that this "cattle killing" is not unique—yet no other such incidents come close to it in scale.

What is important for our study is that this appalling tragedy was one of the stories of defeat told by Joyi, right along with other uplifting, heroic tales of victory. When young Rolihlahla heard this tale, Joyi must have been one of the very last people alive who had been an adult at the time of the cattle killing. "I had yet to realize that the authentic history of our country was not to be found in the books of the British," Mandela wrote later.

This authentic history was transmitted to him by these and other elders' narratives. This living heritage of pain and pride played an essential, early role in forming his conscience. His insistent evocation of his tribal African past during his trials thirty years later are witness to its importance for him.

Mandela would never forget these roots, and neither would the Africans who shouted his name from the rooftops when he walked out of Victor Vester prison on February 11, 1990. If the Afrikaner authorities—who cherish the mystique they have made of their own past—had been more astute, they would have tried to inform themselves about the roots and heritage of this bright, British-trained lawyer, who also happened to be a chief's son, giving him a profound legitimacy in the eyes of his black compatriots. They might have begun to understand that this man represented a unique and powerful confluence of indigenous and modern traditions.

The elders' narratives of military victories and defeats, and of everyday reality, were also accompanied by stories which evoked a more imaginal past, similar to tales of a golden age that occur in

many cultures. And this mythic past which nourished young Rolihlahla's imagination would also nourish the political understanding
of Mandela the activist. Quoting again from his 1962 trial, this is
what he told his white judges so as to explain the origins of his
political ideas, and also to establish the foundation on which a
future South African society should be built:

> The structure and organization of the original African soci-
> eties of this country fascinate me. They have had a great
> influence on my political concepts.

This is clear enough. But he would further clarify the detailed
implications of his thought, imagining a kind of primal commu-
nism, somewhere between a Christian utopian ideal, and that of
a social theorist such as Fourier:

> The land, which was the primary resource in those days,
> belonged to the tribe as a whole. Private property did not
> exist. There were no social classes, no rich and poor, no
> exploiters of other human beings. All men were free and
> equal. This was the guiding principle of government, which
> was also manifest in the organization of the council which
> directed tribal affairs. This council was fully democratic, and
> any member of the tribe could participate in its delibera-
> tions.... This society had many aspects which were primitive
> or undeveloped, and it would not be viable in today's world.
> But it contained the seeds of a revolutionary democracy, with
> no more slavery, servitude, poverty, insecurity, and privation.
> This is the hope which sustains me and my friends in our
> struggle.[25]

---

[25] Nelson Mandela, in his 1964 speech at the Rivonia trial in Pretoria.
Formerly in print in English, under the title of *I Am Prepared to Die;* still in
print under the French title *L'Apartheid*, with a letter by Breyten Breytenbach, Editions de Minuit, Paris, 1965, 1985.

This is perhaps Mandela's clearest formulation of the connection between his Xhosa past and his ideals for modern South Africa. And ever since his liberation from prison and his election to the presidency of the Republic, seemingly worlds away from his trials of the 1960s, he has held to these ideals in his political discourse and in his search for a true democracy.

Now we can see how deeply the young Rolihlahla was affected by his experience at Jongintaba's court during his formative years.

The Transkei where Rolihlahla was born and grew up forms a sort of large irregular rectangle on the map, aligned southwest by northeast. It is bordered on one side by the Indian Ocean and on the other by the mountains of Stormberg and Drakensberg. On its northwest end, the Umzimkulu River forms the traditional border with Natal. To the southwest, the border with the Cape colony was originally the Fish River, pushed by colonists to the Kei River in the nineteenth century. This rectangle measures about 140 by 110 miles, with an area roughly the size of Belgium. The land rises steadily from the coast to the mountains. Dry winds make for low rainfall in the coastal area. Just beyond a narrow, sparsely inhabited coastal band, the inland villages begin, scattered among very green hills. The average population density is less than thirty-five people per square mile. Other than Umtata, the capital, which counts 50,000 inhabitants, its largest towns have populations of less than 5,000. The only big towns nearby are Butterworth and Cofimvaba further south, Bizana and Mount Fletcher to the north, and Port Saint Johns on the coast, at the mouth of the Umzimvuba River, a town which lacks a port, near where the Portuguese ship, the *São João,* sank in 1552.

In 1930, Xhosa-speaking Africans numbered just under three million. Many of these were men between the ages of eighteen and forty, who worked in the mines in Johannesburg and lived in ghettos such as Alexandra or Sophiatown. The traumatic events of the nineteenth century brought profound changes in the economy and social life of the Transkei, and these changes were in full swing at the time Rolihlahla was listening to Joyi's stories. Then came the creation of apartheid in 1948, which led to the Transkei being declared an autonomous homeland in 1976, precipitating a transformation of the entire territory.

However, the first democratic government abolished all this in 1994. The four provinces that made up apartheid South Africa were divided and redistributed into nine new provinces that integrated the former homelands. Now the Transkei is a part of the Eastern Cape Province. This includes the former Ciskei, as well as the eastern parts of the former Cape Province. Its capital is Bisho, former capital of Ciskei. Xhosa-speakers make up over 80 percent of the more than six million people in this new province.

But during Rolihlahla's childhood and adolescence, this little piece of the Transkei was still an insular, traditional world that had managed to remain outside the direct impact of the upheavals of history. In 1930, it experienced the great economic and political changes more as aftershocks.

The Pastor's Daughter

Rolihlahla was entering a new stage in his life, and there were new games to learn. In a letter written from prison in 1985, Mandela recalls his youth at Mqekezweni, and speaks of games with his friends. He adds that he also learned how to court girls. Adolescent preoccupations in this isolated Transkei village were no different from those prevalent in human societies everywhere—the forms and protocols for meeting and associating with the opposite sex.

Rolihlahla was especially susceptible to the charms of Winnie[26] Maryolo, one of the pastor's daughters. They would exchange glances when they saw each other at church, and this led to their meeting and taking walks together in the fields, away from the other villagers. One can imagine them disappearing into the mimosa groves. Mandela notes in his memoirs that Winnie was in love with him.

European missionaries, so often obsessed by sexual problems, had already made clear their violent condemnation of romantic relationships between young Africans. In 1931, when Winnie and Rolihlahla's love affair had begun to bloom, John Henderson Soga dealt with this subject in his book on the Xhosas. He first cited the definition of the word *u-metsho*, from Kropf's *Kafir-English Dictionary:* "To be sweethearts, to have all manner of impure relations;" to which Soga added the adjective, "sexual." For this Presbyterian missionary

---

[26] Not to be confused with Winnie Mandela, whom he married in 1958.

living at Elliotsdale, some miles from Mqekezweni, *u-metsho* was "the most impure of all habits prevalent among the Bantus."[27] And he went to great lengths to explain that it was in fact a "habit," and by no means a "custom." One Xhosa Christian had reassured him by claiming that "It is not a custom, but an immoral habit. It is a sin which is very widespread, and our law does not recognize it, and in fact condemns it."

These Christian missionaries were generally noted for their aptitude for seeing evil at work everywhere. The fact that two youngsters were allowed to slip away to walk together holding hands was evidence of the corruption of a whole people. Post-Victorian English Protestant ministers must have been shocked by the easygoing tolerance of Xhosa parents in such matters. Yet adolescent sexual behavior in Mqekezweni in 1930 was probably not much different from that in many parts of rural Europe, however loose Transkei morals appeared to be.

Nelson Mandela is very discreet, and quite reserved, in his memoirs regarding this subject. In any case, several obstacles worked against his adolescent crushes. One was the fact that he always felt like a bumpkin in Mqekezweni, because he had come from Qunu. Somehow his status as adopted son of the sovereign chief did nothing to alter this feeling, and even intensified it. For him, Mqekezweni seemed like a metropolis in comparison to the few scattered huts at Qunu. He even described it as a "refined" place. And it was true that the other children sometimes made fun of his shyness and awkwardness, reinforcing his feeling of being ill-bred.

Everything went well at first with Winnie—she was in love with him, and love is blind and forgives all. But things were quite otherwise with her sister, Noma Pondo. She decided that this little yokel was unworthy of a pastor's daughter. It is not impossible that she herself had a crush on Rolihlahla, and was jealous of her sister.

---

[27] Correctly used, the term *Bantu* refers to the largest family of languages of central, eastern, and southern Africa. But in South Africa it came to refer to any black sub-Saharan African, often with racist overtones.

In any case, her remonstrance had no effect on Winnie, so she cleverly invited Rolihlahla to a family dinner. At the table, the young boy discovered to his horror that he was expected to use a knife and fork to eat a chicken wing, something he had no idea how to do. Even we who are familiar with the use of these utensils can sympathize with a novice being given such a difficult task, with all the others watching him: the pastor severely, Winnie fondly, and her sister mockingly; for she knew well that this young bumpkin had never eaten with anything but his hands, and had not yet confronted that marvel of Western civilization, the fork. After several futile attempts to manage the wing with these barbaric instruments, Rolihlahla finally gave up, and, deciding he had nothing left to lose, took the wing in his hands and ate it the way he always had.

But this fiasco did not lessen Winnie's love for him. It was the circumstances of life itself which would separate them. She was sent to a school where she would train to become a teacher and Rolihlahla was sent to boarding school at Clarkesbury, a small mission town west of the Bashee River, only twelve miles away as the crow flies, but over forty miles north via the Engcobo road.

During all his years at Mqekezweni, Rolihlahla practically never visited Qunu, where his mother still lived. This is strange, since he was deeply attached to his mother, with whom he had spent his entire life previous to this. The distance between the two villages was not far—in fact, Nosekeni made the long trip to Johannesburg in 1964 to attend her son's trial. Why, then, was this separation between them so brutal? There seem to have been several reasons for this.

First, Rolihlahla adapted well to life with Jongintaba's family. Justice, who was very much like an older brother to him, played an important role in this. Secondly, in Thembu rural society, any public display of a deep emotion such as love for one's mother must always be kept very private and discreet. And finally, the Regent himself did not approve of frequent visits to Qunu by the boy. After all, Rolihlahla was of royal blood on his father's side. He was now an adopted member of the chief's family, and it was not seemly for him to frequent a backwater like Qunu. Someday he would become a counselor of the next Thembu king, and he must behave in a way befitting his rank. Thus Rolihlahla remained in Mqekezweni, observing the ways of Thembu power. Much later, at high school and university, he would learn how to fulfill his destined role.

Yet there were times when he was a little sad and homesick. When Jongintaba perceived this, he would get in his old Ford and drive to Qunu to fetch Nosekeni. She would then spend several days in Mqekezweni with her growing son, who changed so fast she sometimes found it hard to recognize him. But it was not long before she began to miss her kraal and her life at Qunu. She would wander, shy and intimidated, between the Big House and the church, while her son was at school. After a week (or sometimes less) had passed, she would ask the Regent to take her back home. If he was gone, she would walk back over the fields. When saying goodbye to her son, she would take him awkwardly in her arms and embrace him. He would watch her go with the nostalgia of someone watching his own childhood vanish. He would feel sadness for the rest of the day. But the next morning he was running in the fields with Justice and the other boys.

Very soon he would experience one of the decisive events of his life, catapulting him into adolescence, and in a sense, even into adulthood.

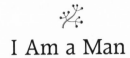

I Am a Man

During Rolihlahla's summer vacation of 1934, he found himself with Justice, Jongintaba's son, Sabata, son of the deceased King Jongilizwe and himself future King of the Thembus, and other chiefs' sons who lived in Mqekezweni. They were preparing for perhaps the most important ceremony in the life of a Xhosa: the initiation ritual, and its culminating moment of circumcision.

This ritual is widespread all over southern Africa. It symbolizes the passage from childhood to adulthood. Usually, this ceremony (which lasted three weeks in 1934) is organized so as to take place when the king's son is about twenty years old. He is accompanied by his friends and the sons of other chiefs. This particular group contained twenty-six youths of varying ages. Following tradition, they spent this entire period in two reed huts on the banks of the Bashee River. This was a traditional spot of initiation of Thembu chiefs, known as Tyhalrha. It was not that far from the kraal at Mwezo where Rolihlahla was born. But it was well away from any other habitations, for no woman must lay eyes upon them.

These twenty-six boys were to live mostly by themselves here, undergoing rituals of both purification and initiation. The religious aspect was strong, and they were constantly reminded by their mentors of the link each of them must maintain between the spirits of the ancestors and the responsibilities they would have as future chiefs.

John Ross, a missionary of the latter half of the nineteenth century, wrote:

When a Xhosa youth has completed the rites, he is supposed to have established a true relationship with the spirits of the ancestors. The elders then speak to each of them, and say: "Now you are a man. It is up to you to make sure that your mother's kettle is never empty."

This is actually a proverbial formula, invoking a man's religious duty after the death of his father to ensure that his mother does not live in want or dishonor. If he fails in this duty, he is considered to be a man without honor, "a nonentity." Such a person is then shunned by respectable people for fear that his company will bring bad luck.

All agree that this ritual is a crucial event in a young man's life. Nelson Mandela writes in his autobiography:

> An uncircumcised Xhosa man is a contradiction in terms, because he is considered to be like a child, not a man. For Xhosas, circumcision represents formal acceptance of a man into their society.

However, the upheavals this society had undergone during the previous century had also affected this ritual. In the old days, it lasted from three to six months. Now it was only three weeks during summer vacation from school.

At the end of the twentieth century, (the time of the writing), the ritual still survives, but its material conditions are greatly changed. For example, in the vast ghettos of Johannesburg and Cape Town, the isolated reed huts are replaced by plastic shelters built under freeway overpasses. Some circumcisions even take place in the hospital.

Yet the initiation still retains the quality of a kind of second birth. In traditional Xhosa society, one's age was typically indicated by naming an event around the time of one's birth. For example, one might say, "I was born in the year of Nongqause." But after initiation, one indicates one's age by naming a chief in one's circumcision group. Nelson Mandela says that he counted his age as a man from the time of his circumcision. Thus he might indicate his age by saying, "I was circumcised with Justice Dalindyebo."

When Jongintaba originally set the day for circumcision, three other things had also to be decided. First came the choice of the *um-nini,* the man whose kraal would host the festivities associated with the initiation. The father of Banabakhe Blayi was chosen because his kraal was nearest to the initiation site, and also because his son was in the group. Then the *i-tonto* (huts) of the *abakweta* (the initiates) were constructed, and a guardian, called the *i-khankatha,* was chosen for the youths during their period of isolation. This was an important role, for this man was not only charged with seeing to the needs of the youths but with initiating them into the mysteries reserved for adulthood.

Sexual questions were prominent in the conversations that took place with him. In the original tradition, the guardian would explain that they must rid themselves of the last traces of boyhood as soon as possible after their period of isolation. In order to do this, they must have sexual relations with a woman who had no man. It could be with a widow, or with an abandoned woman, known as an *idikazi.* Any young man who failed to accomplish this would risk having weak and unhealthy children later on. "This is the worst thing about the circumcision rite," wrote the Reverend John Henderson Soga in 1931. Nelson Mandela does not mention whether this practice was still followed when he was initiated in 1934.

Before leaving Jongintaba's kraal to undergo their initiation, his wife Makhulu placed a sacred necklace around each boy's neck. Known as *ubu-lunga,* it was woven of hairs from a cow's tail, and would keep them in good health and protect them from evil influences in the weeks to come.

On the eve of the group's departure, a celebration took place in the kraal of the *um-nini* (host). A special bull, uncastrated and completely white, had been sacrificed for the occasion. The meat was first offered to the ancestors, and then shared in a great banquet by the twenty-six boys and the others present. This large feast was because of the presence of the King's son in the group. An ordinary initiation group would only involve small family banquets.

When the boys had eaten the sacrificial beef, they removed their old clothes and received a large new piece of cloth, sometimes a skin called a *kaross,* to be worn like a robe.

Before they set off the next day for the straw huts on the Bashee River, the guardian spoke to them, reminding them that initiation means leaving childhood behind for good, and that from that point on they must behave with the dignity of adults. Henceforth, they would no longer quarrel or fight with each other. All the future adults listened to him earnestly. Only two days earlier, they had followed a very different sort of custom. This requires each boy to accomplish some sort of exploit before the initiation, in order to demonstrate his worthiness to become a man. In the old days, this might involve an organized battle with youths from another tribe, or even a raid and theft of cattle. But times had changed.

In his memoirs, Nelson Mandela admits that by his own era the exploits had become somewhat degraded, more mischief than martial deeds. He and his proud young warrior friends had opted for the exploit of stealing an old pig from a villager. They then killed and roasted it under the stars, far from the village. However, he writes that he has a pleasant memory of this event: "No pork has ever tasted so good to me as on that night," he confesses.

The circumcision ceremony took place at noon. All the adult male relatives, including Jongintaba, watched from some distance away, along the river. The twenty-six boys formed a line. They laid their robes on the ground and sat on them with legs spread apart. Rolihlahla was the fifth in line. Like his fellows, he was afraid—afraid of pain, of bringing dishonor on himself and his family by screaming or crying like a child, and in general of not being equal to the challenge of becoming a man. He was sixteen years old.

Then an elder spread butter or animal fat over their heads and bodies. From the corner of his eye, Rolihlahla saw an old man approaching. This was the *ngcibi*, the specialist who would do the actual cutting. He had been summoned from Gcalekaland, to the southwest, near the Kei River. His instrument was his finely sharpened spear.

When any group included a chief's son, the custom was to take measures to prevent his blood from being ritually polluted by being the first to fall on the ground. This is why Justice Bambilanga, son of the sovereign chief, was second in line. The first boy did not belong to the family of a chief, and the *ngcibi* would begin with him. Hence the first blood to fall would be that of a commoner, which would protect the blood of the chiefs' sons from pollution, and also from being used later in any attempt at sorcery.

Rolihlahla suddenly heard the first boy cry out the ritual formula: "I am a man." Very soon afterwards, he heard Justice cry out, but in his voice he could hear the shrill tones of a boy. Rolihlahla became more afraid, but things were happening very swiftly. Suddenly the *ngcibi* was there in front of him. "I felt as if fire was surging through my veins," he said later. Several seconds passed before he remembered to cry out "I am a man."

And so he became one. He had taken the primary step in every Xhosa man's life. After this, he could marry, found a household, and work his own field.

After circumcision, each initiate received a new name. In the old society, this replaced the previous given name he had borne from childhood. Thus the man who had been named Rolihlahla at birth and Nelson at school now became *Dalibunga*. This was a name that traditional Xhosas would prefer over his previous given names. It so happens that Dalibunga means "founder of the Bunga"—the Bunga being the new administration of the Transkei which had been established by the whites a few years before. Thus it would seem that Nelson Mandela's whole career was strangely summed up in this transition: Rolihlahla, "creator of problems" now became Dalibunga, "founder of the new power."

The *ngcibi's* assistant gathered up each severed foreskin, and fastened it to a corner of the initiate's robe. When the ceremony was completed for the whole group, the young men, now considered to be *abakweta,* or initiates, went back inside the two huts, where a small fire had been lit by the *i-khankatha,* or guardian. He placed some green leaves on the coals, generating a pungent smoke. This smoke would aid the healing of the youths' wounds. It was also a kind of echo of the "baptism" that had taken place at birth—for this entry into adulthood was indeed regarded as a kind of second birth.

The huts also contained some leaves of two evergreen species (*isi-ove* and *i-ndlebe-yemuvu*), known for their healing properties, especially in helping scar tissue to form.

One of the tasks of the *i-khankatha* was to make sure each boy's scarring took place without problems. Each day he would personally change the bandage made from medicinal leaves, until healing was complete.

When they returned to the reed huts after the ceremony, the initiates covered their bodies with a layer of white clay, resembling chalk. This would be constantly reapplied when necessary, so as to remain covered from head to toe. It was for this reason that Europeans who happened to catch sight of such youth called them "the white children."

Well before the beginning of the initiation period, the women had prepared special costumes for the boys' dances after circumcision. These were composed of a kind of skirt or toga and a headdress made of long, dried leaves with a long willow branch extending like an antenna from its top. It covered the whole face like a mask so that the dancer could see without being seen. In these costumes, the young men looked much like a swarm of giant grasshoppers. One of the important movements in the dance was when they would suddenly bend their upper bodies downwards in a graceful gesture so that their "antennae" touched the ground, and then quickly stand up straight again.

The only breaks in this period were when Rolihlahla/Dalibunga and his companions would make special trips to the village to perform their costumed dances in kraals where they had been invited.

Abakweta (initiates) standing next to the initiation huts

Abakweta in dance costume

Otherwise, their time was spent in isolation by the huts at Tyhalarha, near the river. Thirteen slept in each hut, which measured only five yards in diameter.

The very first night after circumcision they were awakened late by the guardian. Without enthusiasm, they all got up and left the warmth of the shelter for the cold and humid outdoors. They had to bury their foreskins, and this had to be done in an anthill or termite mound. Thus they would be devoured by the insects and prevented from falling into the hands of any sorcerers.

Dalibunga buried his own foreskin with gravity and nostalgia. "We were symbolically burying our youth. I sensed that I was now abandoning the last vestiges of my childhood." The symbolic significance of such moments is so strong that it can never be forgotten. Nothing could ever erase the bond he felt with this place of initiation, whose earth he had literally nourished with a part of himself. A part of his own body had been torn away and sacrificed so as to discover and release his adult sexuality. Dalibunga's childhood was indeed buried along with his foreskin in this earth, in the same motherland as the kraal of his birth. Whatever trials life might have in store for him as an adult, he knew that he could always return to this primal source, his deepest roots, and find renewal there. Even the walls and barbed wire of the white man's prisons could not break this connection.

During the first week, the *abakweta* were only allowed to eat cold bullion made from corn. Fresh vegetables, fruit, and meat were forbidden. The *i-khankatha* himself served their food with a wooden spoon. It was as if they had to begin all over again in order to become men after this second birth. After a week had passed, an animal was sacrificed and they ate roasted meat. They shared cornbread that had been smoked and roasted. Its crust was blackened, and it contained traditional medicines inside. They would chew this bread thoroughly, and then spit mouthfuls out in the four cardinal directions.

For the next three weeks, the young men remained in complete isolation from the community. The only exceptions were certain evenings when they were ceremonially invited to a kraal. They went there to perform dances, dressed in their insect-like costumes, faces painted white, bodies wrapped in blankets. No woman was supposed to set eyes upon them. But times have changed since then. So much so that in January, 1990, while driving along the National Highway 30 to Grahamstown, between the Transkei and the Ciskei, my wife and I caught sight of three young *abakweta* sitting on a stone wall bordering a pasture. They were waving and gesturing to passing cars. Their faces were covered with the ritual white paint, but they did not wear the traditional blankets. They also wore shorts. My wife's presence obviously did not bother them. We responded to their waving with big waves of our own. This made them burst into laughter. Indeed, times have changed—yet the initiation ritual survives.

During this isolation period in more traditional times, one of the principal taboos regarded the boys' language. They were forbidden to speak the common language, and had to use a special pseudo-secret language in which major common words were replaced by ritual words. These words are specific to this type of initiation, and have been catalogued by ethnologists. Here are a few examples:

English	Xhosa	Initiation word
corn	um-bona	iz-agweba
livestock	in-komo	in-jima
water	ama-nzi	ama-cam
spoon	i-cepe	i-dada
calf	i-tole	i-qele
boy	i-kwenkwe	i-bengeta
woman	um-fazi	isi-gqwati
girl	in-tombi	in-tshiki
dog	in-ja	i-kanka
clothing	in-gubo	izi-nqwashu
milk	ama-si	ama-rola

In addition to these traditional "secret" words, the *abakweta* invented their own genuinely secret words, unique to their initiation group. Long after the initiation period was over, and the young men had returned to normal life, they would continue to use these initiation words with each other, particularly when they did not want outsiders to understand their conversation. It is interesting to note that this custom is actually an amplified form of a universal, often spontaneous practice which occurs among human societies everywhere: when a group of people become isolated from the main community, and undergo special experiences together (it could be something as ordinary as a vacation colony, a club, a fraternity, etc.), they not infrequently develop a special vocabulary, and in some cases even a mock language. This may consist of only a few words—perhaps even a single nonsense word, joke, or story. But when these people get together again, this special language is a powerful means of evoking and reliving experiences which only they can fully appreciate.

For these twenty-six young *abakweta*, their new language was a means of participating in tradition, yet it was also a means of separating and distinguishing themselves forever from the larger community, including their own mentors. These unique group languages only consisted of a few dozen words, and are known generically as *hlonipa*, which means "shyness, discretion, respect." Even as mature adults, they might resort to it when meeting old friends from their group, especially in the presence of women.

During the day, the initiates would take long walks in the hills, watching the changing spectacle of nature and wildlife (today, they walk to the highway and watch passing cars). They formed small groups and shared stories and feelings about their lives—the lives they were leaving forever, and the new ones that awaited them as men. For the Xhosa peoples, this transition was far more than just a change of age and activity.

Childhood had been village life, herding animals, and the family circle. For boys of noble blood, it was also the Regent's court, and its lessons in power and social responsibility. For all the boys, childhood had been especially their African tradition. No matter how influential the white administrators and missionaries, their childhood had been their deepest link to the past centuries of their culture, including this initiation. Whether their future as adults would be as African was much more in doubt. For most of them, manhood would turn out to be a progressive, grievous loss of this tradition. Some of them had already taken the first step in this direction: for example, Banabakhe Blayi, whose father played the role of host of this initiation group, had already begun working at a job in a gold mine in Johannesburg. He was the only one of the abakweta who had been to the mythical city of *eGoli* (derived from the English word "gold"). He regaled the others with stories of his fortunes and adventurous life for the short time he had been there. Of course he didn't mention the men's hostels where the workers lived, crowded flophouses of misery and violence. Nor did he speak of the cruelty of the petty white overseers, or the humiliating searches after long days picking and digging for pieces of gold ore at the bottom of a dark hole. Instead, he proudly showed them some coins and paper money he had earned, which they looked upon with wonder. Money was rare among them, and this was clearly impressive proof of all that Banabakhe had been telling them. As Mandela wrote, "His stories of the gold mines excited us so much that I was almost ready to believe that being a miner was better than being a king."

But Rolihlahla knew that this was not his destiny. He would be an advisor to King Sabata, and so he was sent to boarding school. Nevertheless, the seeds planted by Banabakhe continued to grow. Years later, he actually went to Johannesburg and tried the mines of *eGoli* for himself. It was not without bitterness that he wrote: "It was much later that I realized how many young men were deceived by stories such as Banabakhe's, which convinced them that their salvation lay in the Johannesburg mines. It was with their health and their lives that they paid for this illusion. In those days,

working in the mines was almost as powerful a symbol of passage
into manhood as circumcision. This myth helped the owners of
the mines, but not my people."

These twenty-six young men, caught between two cultural
worlds, dreaming of a different life and a different world, were
unaware of the danger they faced. Even as they practiced their initiation rites, decisions were being made by honorable Christian
gentlemen in the distant councils of Pretoria and Cape Town which
would cast a pall over their adult lives. The world being built by
these authorities was a world in which they had no place as human
beings. Only one of them, Rolihlahla, would decide that, because
the world had no place for him, the world must change.

But none of these concerns could contaminate the sacred, time-
less atmosphere of the initiation period. It was a time for deep
reflection for Rolihlahla. From time to time, older men from the
village would visit the *abakweta,* and notice his silhouette against
the sky, standing apart from the rest of the group, covered with his
blanket, white paint on his face making his eyes even darker, lost
in contemplation. He felt the seriousness and sadness of this
moment, which was the last summer vacation of childhood.

Already, he sensed something of his destiny, for he took very
seriously the vow to "make sure your mother's kettle is never
empty." He also took seriously the ideal of service that he learned
in the best teachings of the white man's school. Something told
him that he could not separate his mother's welfare from that of
his people as a whole. Thirty years later, he declared to his judges:

> At that time I hoped that life would offer me an opportunity
> to serve my people, and add my small contribution to their
> struggle for freedom. This determined all my actions since
> that time, including those related to the accusations brought
> against me in this trial.

For Nelson Mandela, this is what it meant to be a man and take care of his mother. How could these white judges understand this man and his actions? Their view of him as a member of an inferior race prevented them from seeing that he was acting like idealistic youth in all cultures everywhere, who have come of age amidst social and cultural rupture. Such youths devote themselves with passion to healing the cultural and psychological fracture in their lives, whether through political dissent, artistic creation, or humanitarian action. But even aside from the blindness of their racism, perhaps what really baffled his judges was what drives a man to remain loyal to something in his childhood and his ancestral tradition, something which is in danger of being betrayed. Is it guilt, love, or loyalty that drives a gifted young man to refuse the advantages offered him by an oppressor, and work to prevent the cultural rupture from becoming a betrayal? This is a question that can never be answered definitively.

As Rolihlahla walked slowly and solemnly back toward the *abakweta* huts on the Bashee River, his body covered with white clay, he made a silent vow. No matter what kind of adult he became (advisor to the Thembu king, miner, or—who knows?—maybe even a lawyer), this much was certain: he would never betray his childhood or allow his mother's kettle to go empty. And this is a promise he kept, though not in any way he could foresee.

A few days before the end of the initiation period, the guardian came and shaved the young men's heads. After a few days more of waiting for a stubble to grow back, they all bathed ceremonially in the river. It was a joyous occasion for them, and they held a race to see who jumped in the river first, for he would be named man of the day. The dried clay covering came off their bodies in large plaques, turning the water into a boisterous mudpool. After thoroughly washing themselves, they dried off in the sun. But they discovered that a gray film still remained on their bodies, making further washings necessary. Finally, when the long bath was over, they prepared to return to the community.

There was one last ritual to be performed before they set off. The *i-khankatha* had returned and painted their bodies with red clay. Then a large fire was built near the river, and the straw huts where they had been living for three weeks were burned. Their dance costumes and ritual robes were also thrown into the fire. Then they all started for home, looking fixedly ahead of them. The guardian had admonished them not to look even once at the smoldering remains behind them. They walked with their eyes straight ahead, toward the kraal of Banabakhe Blayi's father, for the feast of the last day.

Ancient tradition enjoined these red-painted young men to find a girl that very night, make love with her, and marry her later. Such a young bride was known as "she who wipes off the red clay." But times had long since changed. This custom was rarely followed anymore, at least not in this ancient form. Nelson Mandela relates in his autobiography that it was necessary to rub his skin with fat in order to remove the red clay, but he is discreet about what else happened that night.

The feast at the kraal was both solemn and joyous. They ate roasted meat and drank *u-tywala*, a beer brewed from fermented corn. They also listened to speeches and tales. The Regent Jongintaba was there, and reminded them that they must conduct themselves from now on with the reserve and wisdom befitting their status as men. Then Chief Meligqili, one of Jongilizwe Dalindyebo's sons, made an unexpected, impassioned speech that Rolihlahla would never forget. He denounced the rule of the white man, which was destroying the dignity and well-being of the Xhosas and other South African peoples. "We have become slaves in our own land," he said. He lamented the fact that these young men before him had little or no chance of following the ways of their ancestors and becoming either herdsmen (the whites had confiscated too much Xhosa land), chiefs (the whites had taken away their power), warriors (the whites had superior weapons and had confiscated theirs), or students and teachers of their own tradition (for they had no schools of their own). Instead, Chief Meligqili said, "From now on, young men will cough their lungs out in the bowels of the earth, working in the white man's mines, never seeing the sun, ruining their health so that a few whites can live in fabulous wealth."

The newborn young men listened to him with shock and bewilderment. No one else had talked to them in this way, not even the old men. Surely Meligqili's words were a sign of his own bitterness and pessimism. These youths, filled with the glowing legends of *eGoli,* simply could not accept, could not really even hear, this man's warnings. And he concluded his speech with these sad and terrible words: "The children of *Ngubengcuka* are dying." Even young Rolihlahla was offended by this discourse. "This petty chief had ruined my day and hurt my pride with these perverse remarks," Nelson Mandela later admitted. But this minor chieftain's wise and potent words would remain as seeds within him, germinating and flowering years later. The time would come when he would look at himself and see the extent of his own ignorance.

The next day, when the fires of the feast had been extinguished, and the many words he had heard ceased to echo in his mind, Rolihlahla walked alone back toward the Bashee River. Looking at it, he realized that he had never even crossed this river. What did he know about the world? All that remained of their huts were two piles of ashes. At the camp, he saw the grass still flattened by their dances, and the black circles left by their fires. He looked in silence, hearing the sound of the river. "I was already in mourning for my vanished youth," he would write later. It would be very hard to find his place in the world beyond this river.

The World Opens

In February 1934 (the beginning of the school year in the southern hemisphere), the sixteen-year-old Rolihlahla sat beside the Regent Jongintaba at the wheel of his Ford V8. They were headed for the boarding school at Clarkesbury. It was Rolihlahla's first crossing of the Bashee River, and his eyes were wide open, taking in everything. He was wearing heavy leather boots, which he had carefully polished the night before. Little did he know that these big, shiny boots would only brand him as a country bumpkin at his new school, making the girls giggle when he stomped along the wooden floor of the classroom, causing it to shake.

Clarkesbury School was founded in 1825 by Methodist missionaries, on land donated by King Ngubengenka, a Thembu ancestor of Rolihlahla's. In spite of his rustic manners, he was received royally at the school, in honor of his ancestry. He admits in his biography that this caused him to be a bit conceited at first. But this did not last long, for he had to work hard to keep up at school. He claims he was barely even average in both studies and sports, but this is almost certainly an exaggeration due to his great modesty in later life.

On the drive to Clarkesbury, the Regent admonished young Rolihlahla to behave with the dignity befitting a member of his family, someone whose destiny was to become an advisor to King Sabata. Rolihlahla watched the rolling, grassy hills of the Transkei pass by on both sides of the road, punctuated by mimosa forests. Large herds of animals seemed small and lost in the immensity of the meadows. Sometimes groups of children played at throwing stones, startling flocks of birds, or chased after the car, laughing. It had only been a few days since he had stood in deep reflection beside the Bashee River, staring at the "pyramids of ashes" of the initiation huts with a prophetic sense of mourning his childhood. Now, as the old Ford crossed that river, he felt a mysterious, decisive transformation taking place in himself. Did he already sense, on this short drive to Clarkesbury, listening to the Regent's well-intentioned lecturing, that these Transkei hills could not contain his destiny, and that the role of counselor to a petty traditional king would be too limited a role for him? In any case, this hour-long drive was a major turning point in his life—as significant as the long walk with his mother over the fields from Qunu to Mqekezweni when he was nine years old. He could not have known that he would never return to live in his native Transkei hills, and that he would only visit his native village once or twice in the next several decades. From now on, the scenery of his life would be increasingly dominated by the white man's world of modern South Africa. Even today, he feels that he can never really settle in the house he has built at Mqekezweni, except for weekends and vacations.

After arriving at the school, he shook hands for the first time in his life with a white person. The hand was that of the Reverend Harris. Jongintaba had spoken to him about this man, whose devotion to indigenous peoples had earned him the title of "the white Thembu." The Regent himself had been a student of his in his youth. Before leaving to drive back to Mqekezweni, he gave Nelson a one-pound note. The youth was greatly impressed. He had never really needed money in the village, and this was by far the largest sum he had ever possessed.

Nelson adapted quickly to life at the Methodist boarding school; but it was not easy. "Clarkesbury was run more like a military academy than an institution for training future teachers," he later wrote. Reverend Harris was a severe and formidable taskmaster. Everyone stood up when he entered the room, even the white teachers. The boys slept in a dormitory room with forty beds. But the school's curriculum and discipline were not that different from a typical English boarding school of the period. In spite of this austerity, and notwithstanding his own modest disclaimers, Nelson Mandela obtained his first diploma in two years, instead of the usual three.

Life at the school also included chores, one of which was working in the garden. Because of young Nelson's noble status, Reverend Harris arranged for him to work in his own personal garden. This experience was to have an important effect, leading to a lifelong love of gardening. It also brought two new joys into young Nelson's life: getting to know the Reverend, who turned out to be a simple, honest, warm-hearted man; and his wife, who brought delicious little hotcakes to the boy while he was working. Mandela later joked that her kindness and hotcakes were probably the main reason he learned to love gardening.

Many years later, at Robben Island, the prisoner would beg the authorities for years before finally obtaining the right to dig a small garden alongside the wall in the courtyard. This was unheard of, and the other prisoners teased him, saying he must be a miner at heart because he spent so much of his free time picking and shoveling the rocky soil. The guards found seeds for him—a kindness which they never had occasion to regret, for his garden produced large quantities of onions and tomatoes, some of which he regularly offered to them.

In March of 1982, Nelson Mandela and his Rivonia colleagues were transferred from Robben Island to Pollsmoor prison, just southwest of Cape Town. The white Afrikaner dissident poet and writer Breyten Breytenbach was also serving time in this prison at that time, but the two men never met inside the walls. The Rivonia group was housed in a large space on a roof of one of the buildings inside. They also had access to a large courtyard, about the size of half a football field, but covered with pavement. It was a world surrounded by concrete, and Mandela keenly missed his garden and the natural setting of Robben Island. Again he petitioned the authorities for permission to dig a garden, but this time it was readily accepted. One of the secret reasons for transferring these prisoners was because Pollsmoor was a place where white political authorities of ministerial rank could meet with Nelson Mandela more discreetly than at Robben Island. This was the beginning of what would become outright negotiations years later. Since there was no unpaved ground available for his garden there, he requested, and was given, a quantity of good soil and sixteen large oil drums, each of which he sawed in two. Filled with the soil, he thus obtained "thirty-two giant flower pots." He used these to plant onions, eggplant, cauliflower, carrots, and broccoli. In hat and gloves, he worked for two hours every morning in his garden, or "small farm," as he jokingly called it, which at one time counted almost 900 producing plants. His garden was a bright spot in prison life, and as before, he offered fresh vegetables to the guards as well as to the other prisoners.

His later words on this experience are also an eloquent statement about freedom and confinement: "In prison, a garden is one of the few things you can really master and call your own. Planting a seed, watching it grow, caring for it, and finally enjoying its fruits is a simple but lasting satisfaction. The feeling of being the steward of this tiny patch of earth is a small taste of freedom."

Breyten Breytenbach, who spent his childhood in the country a few miles north of Cape Town, was also a prison gardener, but he was only allowed a flower bed with some roses and carnations. When he discretely planted some tomatoes, the warden found out about by intercepting a letter Breytenbach wrote to his mother, and ordered the plants torn out.

Other than gardening, one of young Nelson's passions at Clarkesbury was sports. The boys played barefoot soccer in the dust. They also built their own makeshift tennis racquets and played on the lawns with short grass. This was the beginning of a love of tennis which also found expression in prison at Robben Island, where the inmates obtained authorization to paint lines for a tennis court on the concrete. When they finally were able to put up a net, they played with a passion, as if practicing for Wimbledon. "I had a good forehand and a poor backhand," he wrote. "I played the back of the court, only going to the net when I had an easy shot."

At Clarkesbury, he also fell in love. The girl was one of those who made fun of his heavy boots and rustic walk. But Mathona, whom he at first called "Miss Know-it-all," turned out to have a sweet nature, as well as being attracted to him. "She was the first girl I ever developed a true friendship with, as equals," he wrote. But he never saw her again after leaving Clarkesbury. Her parents were too poor for her to continue her studies, or for her to keep in touch with the son of a Thembu royal family.

Finishing his diploma after two years at Clarkesbury, he left in 1937 for the Methodist high school at Healdtown. He and Jongintaba left Mqekezweni very early one morning in the old Ford, for this was a much longer trip. They parked the car and caught a train at Butterworth, a large village on the road south from Umtata to East London. They left the train at the Fort Beaufort station, near Healdtown. On this trip, they also crossed the Kei River, the historic border of the Cape colony with the Transkei.

This was the first time the nineteen-year-old Nelson had left the Transkei. Fort Beaufort was a small town built around a fort, which was one of a series of fortified border posts. Like Fort Brown and Fort Willshire, it was built in the mid-nineteenth century, with the mission of defending the original border between the Cape Colony and "Kafirland," established along the Fish River, over one hundred miles west of the Kei River. The Healdtown high school stood at the edge of the small town of Alice, site of Fort Hare, which had been converted into South Africa's first black university.

Both the university and the new high school had been built during World War I by the Methodist Church. The white government offered no aid, nor even its permission. At that time, it was the largest high school for indigenous Africans south of the equator. Young Nelson and his friends were greatly impressed by the headmaster, Arthur Wellington, a descendent of the famous Duke of Wellington. In those days their greatest ambition was to become "black Englishmen."

The discipline at Healdtown was even more military than at Clarkesbury: out of bed at 6:00 A.M., breakfast of dry bread and warm water with sugar at 6:40, underneath the portrait of King George VI. Then, after the 8:00 inspection, they were in class until 12:45 P.M. Lunch consisted of porridge, curds, beans, and rarely meat. Then, afternoon classes until 5:00, sports, supper, required study from 7:00 until 9:00, and lights out at 9:30.

Nelson submitted to this regime, Draconian by contemporary standards, without complaint. He was known as a serious, hardworking boy, who succeeded in his studies with no apparent problems. He was tall and lean, and loved sports, especially long-distance running and boxing.

Although the Xhosas were the largest ethnic group at Healdtown, there were a number of other tribes represented there: Sothos, Mpondos, and students from as far away as Swaziland and Botswana. The boys tended to socialize only among their own group, mixing minimally with members of other tribes. But Nelson Mandela became more and more dissatisfied with this voluntary segregation as time went on. In the classroom, on the playing field, at meals, and in the dormitory, he gradually came to see himself as something much more than a Thembu or a Xhosa: for the first time, he began to see himself as an African. One day he made friends with a Sotho boy named Zachariah Molete. This was so unheard of that he still remembers the pride he felt at what amounted to an act of social audacity. This turned out to be the first in a series of encounters and discoveries which would broaden his horizons and begin to shape his constantly evolving political philosophy. This taboo-breaking friendship at the Healdtown high school was the seed of what ultimately became his famous "rainbow" vision for South Africa, a vision which has now succeeded in winning over people of all colors and ethnic groups there, at least in principle. But of course the young Mandela could have no notion of this. However, he did realize that this friendship was part of his ongoing discovery that the world was vastly more diverse and complex than the simple, reassuring view he had inherited at Mqekezweni. Having left his native Transkei by crossing the Kei and Fish rivers, he was now making the infinitely more difficult crossing of the inner borders of the social identity and conditioning of his childhood.

And this crossing had its challenging moments. One of the most popular teachers was a young Sotho man named Frank Lebentlele, who often participated in sports with the boys. But when he married a young Xhosa woman, it was a terrible shock to all of them. Even Nelson could not help falling momentarily back into, as he put it later, "the tribalism which still imprisoned me." Yet his very observation of this mechanical reaction in himself made him even more determined to break out of it. He became more deeply convinced that he was indeed an African, and not just a Thembu or a Xhosa.

Toward the end of the last year, the Healdtown administration announced that the great Xhosa poet, S.E. Krune Mqhayi, would be visiting the school. The very idea that an important poet could be African, and not English, was somewhat revolutionary to the boys. How could he be legitimate, unless he wrote like Wordsworth, Shelley, or Keats? What other kind of Xhosa would be invited to Healdtown, this island of British culture?

For Nelson and the others, "culture" was something that had nothing to do with their Africa of vast plains and forests, animal herds, straw and clay huts, traditional clothes, and bare feet. How could the serene, interminable councils at traditional courts such as that of the Regent Jongintaba compare with the mighty British parliament? Culture as they had learned it meant the English language, Christian prayers, the portrait of King George looking down upon them every morning, biology, mathematics, and British history. Culture was embodied in the school principal, Dr. Arthur Wellington, a descendent of the great Duke who had defeated Napoleon at Waterloo. The African culture they knew seemed to have as little to do with true culture as ships that pass each other in the night.

For these reasons, the encounter with Krune Mqhayi was "like a comet crossing the sky" to young Nelson. The impact came as soon as the poet entered the hall where the boys were assembled. Not only was he dressed in very traditional African costume—with leopard skin, and even carrying a spear—but even more amazing to the boys was that he entered the room via the door that led to Dr. Wellington's private apartments. Until now, they had never seen anyone but the headmaster use this door. The effect was electrifying. "It was as if the universe had turned upside-down," he wrote.

Mqhayi (1875–1945) is today considered as both founder and greatest figure of Xhosa literature in the first half of the twentieth century. When Mandela saw him in 1938, he was famous in South Africa as a novelist, and even more so as a poet. Especially appreciated are his poems based on *isibongo,* a traditional epic genre of homage to heroes and kings. The poem he read that day at Healdtown school had been written thirteen years before, on the occasion of the visit of the Prince of Wales to South Africa. With irony and daring, the poet addresses the future King of England (he had recently been crowned in 1936, and a rather severe-looking portrait of him hung over the headmaster's door) as follows:

> *Hayi,* O mighty Great Britain!
> You arrive on our shores with a Bible and a bottle.
> You arrive in pairs, a missionary escorted by a soldier.
> You bring gunpowder, rifles, and cannons.
> Excuse me, O my father, but which of these gifts are we to
>   accept?

Following this, Mqhayi advanced toward the audience so that his back was toward Dr. Wellington. He raised his spear, touched the curtain rod with it, and said to the boys: "This spear represents what is glorious and true in African history. It is the symbol of the African as warrior and as artist. This curtain rod is a symbol of Western industry—clever, but cold; intelligent, but soulless." After some more words in this vein, he concluded: "We have been kneeling too long before the false gods of the white man."

Dr. Wellington listened to all this with calm and good humor. And in those days he had reason to be calm, knowing that the neocolonial world he lived in was under the protection of many battalions of faithful British soldiers with overwhelmingly superior arms. The year was 1938, and he was far more concerned about what the Germans were doing in Europe than about African uprisings, which were a thing of the past. Also, he was a guide of minds and souls, not a politician or a warrior. This proud, picturesque Xhosa poet posed no threat to the established order.

But when he had finished, the students rose as one and broke into thunderous applause and shouts of joy. Educators of the established order would do well to take poets more seriously when they move their pupils this deeply.

Like Elegant Young Europeans

In early 1939, the Regent obtained a scholarship from the Bunga so that Nelson could continue his studies at Fort Hare University, only a few miles from Healdtown. A few weeks later, he began the February term at this prestigious establishment. When he was there, it was still considered to be the training ground for the black elite, and remained so until the apartheid regime destroyed its influence. This was accomplished by the clever ruse of requiring that classes be conducted in Xhosa, Zulu, and other native languages, with English forbidden. This immediately reduced it to the status of a school for training Africans who would administer the homelands, barring them from access to the world of white power.

In January, the Regent brought Nelson to Umtata and bought him a three-piece suit, with the fashionable wide lapels worn by young Europeans of the era. We have no way of knowing what clothing stores were like in Umtata in 1939, but on our trip there in 1990, we saw stores displaying Pierre Cardin suits. There were also boutiques vaunting the new African-inspired fashions at high prices. This exotic, upscale mix contrasted violently with the poverty and misery in this city of perpendicular streets, full of potholes, often unpaved and lined with rows of gray, soulless, concrete structures.

But Nelson was delighted with his new suit, and imagined that no one in Fort Hare could be more elegantly dressed than he. He had himself photographed for the occasion—the earliest known photograph of the future President of South Africa (reproduced on the cover of this book). He is standing against a brick wall with

arms crossed, wearing a wristwatch. His look is serious and proud—
the very image of a young "black Englishman." What had become
of Rolihlahla, Nosekeni's son? By the time of this photograph, he
had moved too far from the world of Qunu and Mqekezweni to ever
return. In spite of the seeds sown by Mqhayi, the years at school
spent imbibing British history, literature, language, and customs
had done their work. The poet's seeds were certainly growing in
their own quiet way. Nevertheless, even as a radical reformer, Mandela would retain a lifelong love of European elegance. He would
continue to favor the three-piece suit right up to that day in 1964,
when he had to exchange it for a prison uniform.

When he entered the university in 1939, his adoptive brother Justice, who vastly preferred soccer to studies, had not yet finished high
school at Healdtown, though he and Nelson were the same age.

This institution dated from 1905, just after the end of the Boer
War. The British administration decided to create a central university for indigenous peoples, first known as the Native Central
College. In 1908, Mr. McLaren, who had been sent by the Minister of Education to speak before the Bunga of the Transkei,
declared that "The Minister's goal is to offer natives the same education as Europeans, with the same curricula and the same standards. The reason for this is that many Europeans and Africans will
be working together, and it will be better if they have a common
base of knowledge. If they have different educations, they will not
be able to understand each other."

This speech in 1908 gives pause for reflection. For one thing, its
vision of equal educational opportunity in a common language is
exactly what was later attacked by the decree of the apartheid
National Party in 1960, which required Fort Hare to conduct classes
in indigenous languages. On the other hand, this vision of education had its unspoken limits. Even these liberal British Christians,
who would eventually allow a few of their sons and daughters to mix
with blacks at Fort Hare University, could not yet imagine extending this ideal to allowing blacks to enroll in the white universities

that existed already. This demonstrates that the policy of racial segregation was not just something invented by apartheid in 1948. It
was already a long-established practice, arising out of three centuries
of colonialism. The British were in general far less rigid and more
humane in their practice of it—yet they still practiced it.

The authorities had deliberated long on the choice of a site for
the new black university. Bloemfontein, capital of the Orange Free
State, had been the favorite because of its central location in South
Africa as a whole. But the choice finally settled on the more out-
lying location of Fort Hare, on a bend of the Tyumie River. It was
largely because the land had been donated by the Methodist mission of Lovedale. This mission derived its name from its founder,
John Love. The mission was originally established in the mid-
nineteenth century by the Hoxton Presbyterian Church, known as
the Scottish Church.

Louis Botha, Prime Minister of the Union of South Africa, inau-
gurated the university two years before Rolihlahla's birth. On that
morning of February 8, 1916, the beginning of the school year,
some twenty young men and women stood outside in the summer
sunshine listening to the Prime Minister speak. The new classroom
and other buildings huddled against those of the old fort, forming
an ensemble which seemed like a tiny human island lost in the vast
grassy prairies of the veldt around them. There were eighteen
blacks (two of them women) and two whites, both sons of the
Lovedale missionaries.

A witness described the scene in this way:

> The Prime Minister stood in the shade cast by the canopy of
> a horse carriage. Standing on a hill, with the veldt all around
> him, he solemnly proclaimed the opening of the first uni-
> versity in South Africa for indigenous peoples. He could
> hardly have been unaware of the strangeness of the setting
> for such an inauguration. Looking all around, the only thing
> that broke the immensity of the veldt was this bare hill, with

a few buildings added onto an old fort. The fort had long since lost its warlike aspect, as had the enigmatic hills of the Amatole nearby, formerly a base of African warriors who attacked the fort. Besides this, there were a few old houses on the banks of the Tyumie River, the outlines of a village in the distance—and above all, a group of young people with a great flame of faith burning in their hearts.[28]

Alexander Kerr had arrived from Scotland to take over the direction of Fort Hare University (previously known as Native Central College). He was still running it in 1939 when Mandela arrived, and later retired in 1948. He was a generous-hearted man, well-loved and highly respected throughout his long career. However, his memoirs (from which the above passage is taken) sometimes offer a glimpse of the deeply ambivalent attitude toward blacks of many whites of that era, even the most tolerant. For example, after landing by English ship at East London, he went by train to the town of Alice.

> I remember an impression I had in those days, and which seems a bit naive to me now, especially considering that I was on my way to direct a university for blacks: looking out of the train window, I was simply astonished that we saw so many black people.

What he does not mention here is his wife's feelings, which were not just of surprise, but of fear and anxiety. Before leaving for Africa, Mr. and Mrs. Kerr had set out to educate themselves by reading a "scientific" book entitled *Black and White in South Africa,* by Maurice Evans:

---

[28] Alexander Kerr, *Fort Hare, 1915–1948: The Evolution of an African College* (Pietermaritzburg: Shuterand Shooter, 1968).

I found this book thoroughly remarkable; but I was worried, because in some places it suggested that around the age of puberty, African natives were victims of an "arrested development." Several scientists had explained this by a "premature closing of cranial sutures." Since I could see no point in devoting my efforts to raising the educational level of a race which evidently [...] was physically incapable of benefiting from it, I asked Mr. Schreiner *[an official of the Scottish Church—Ed.]* what he thought about this. I still remember the sense of relief I felt when he declared categorically that he didn't believe a word of it.

And readers today may well feel a sense of relief that the professor was relieved of this notion. But it is significant that even this open-minded, highly educated, thirty-one-year-old European pastor arrived in South Africa in 1916 with such a book in his luggage. It was a book whose popularity persisted, in spite of the fact that it propagated racist, pseudo-scientific theories, which both scientists and political leaders such as Victor Schoelcher had long ago denounced, as early as 1840.

Given this climate, is it any wonder that even an essentially decent man like Alexander Kerr, a product of European Christian civilization, would feel no sense of surprise at the idea of creating a university for blacks—in other words, an institution whose very existence implied that blacks should be barred from attending the already-functioning universities for whites?

On May 9, 1925, in his address at the graduation ceremony, Dr. Henderson, chairman of the University board, dealt with this question squarely:

> How can we justify the establishment of a university reserved for natives? Although racial feelings certainly prompted the decision to have a separate university for natives, this is not a curse, but a decisive advantage. I like to think that we in this country are witness to the establishment of relations

between two brothers of the human race who have long been separated, each following his own way, over millennia. [...] Today, the existence of Fort Hare offers the more backward brother a chance for natural self-development, instead of an unnatural or forced development. Fort Hare has no obligation to meekly follow the white universities, excellent as they may be for their own students. This backward brother is not so lacking in wisdom as to want to act as if he did not possess a personality of his own, a history of his own, racial characteristics of his own, a heritage which arises out of his own racial experience, and his own specific talents, which will enable him to contribute to the human richness of the twentieth century. I would like to propose that you, students at Fort Hare University, become true to yourselves, as people who are a part of God's great plan.

This unctuous 1925 speech is worth noting, for it is a precursor of the arguments for apartheid which were advanced almost thirty years later. It makes use of the same rhetoric of "separate development" used by the racist National Party. This shows to what extent apartheid dogma was not just the outcome of colonial history, as we noted earlier, but also of an explicit ideological preparation, at least part of which was formulated at Fort Hare itself.

Of course, these well-intentioned Methodist pastors at Fort Hare, many of whom sincerely devoted their lives to helping their black students, were totally unaware that they were participating in the ideological construction of a political regime which was in stark contradiction to their own interpretation of the Gospels. They were blind to the fact that this policy of educational segregation was helping to prepare the justification for a regime which would bring South Africa to the brink of chaos. When Alexander Kerr wrote his memoirs in 1968, he still showed no signs of misgiving about the notion of "separate education," even in the midst of the scandalous misery and oppression of the apartheid regime.

Such was the mindset of the mentors under whom Nelson Mandela began his university studies. He studied English (which he had not yet learned to speak fluently), anthropology, political science, law, and native administration. This last subject was indicative of the career that had already been planned for him: an administrative official in indigenous territories, destined to become separate homelands. The overall atmosphere left little doubt as to the place of blacks in relation to whites. Granted, there had been some progress—in 1939, whites showed more respect for black students than they had in previous generations. But to get an idea of the context and nature of this "progress," and of the climate which led to Nelson Mandela's departure from Fort Hare in 1941, it is instructive to consider the state of race relations only a few years previous to his arrival there.

In 1925, Dr. Henderson made a speech to his colleagues, the other white professors, as follows:

> The students here should be treated as adults. Also, the widespread use of the word "boy" applied to native adult males manifests a subtle attitude of condescension. So this should be taken into account in all relationships within the university.

Note the use of the word "subtle" here. Dr. Henderson cannot have been unaware of the fact that "boy" was a synonym for house servant. For adult African males who were not house servants, this word applied to them was anything but subtle. Furthermore, he only says this should be "taken into account," not that the practice should be eliminated. This little speech says much about prevalent attitudes of whites in those days.

Given his background and temperament, how could Nelson Rolihlahla Mandela have failed to be offended by such attitudes? Proud of his identity as a Thembu, a Xhosa, and now beginning to see himself an African, to encounter such condescension, "subtle" or not, as a student in this temple of learning, led to a disillusionment in his own attitude toward whites. It seemed they were the same here as they were everywhere. Just as with the petty magistrate at Mvezo who had humiliated his father, these university whites seemed to have the same old arrogance, based on a belief in their own superiority to blacks. Whether their words were gentle or harsh, they were all convinced that their civilization, their history, and their ideas of justice, humanity, and God were the only true, definitive, and universal ones.

At Fort Hare, Mandela was reunited with a number of students he had known at Clarkesbury and at Healdtown, who graduated a year or so behind him. But, in the grand tradition of all British schools, upperclassmen do not fraternize with underclassmen, and the future Thembu royal advisor stuck to his own. However, he made an exception with Kaiser Matanzima, who was his uncle, despite being younger. The nephew took the uncle under his protection, securing a place for him in Wesley House, his own residence hall. Destiny was to take them in dramatically opposed directions, for Matanzima would capitulate twenty-five years later to apartheid and become President of the puppet Transkei "independent" homeland.

Living conditions in 1939 at Fort Hare had improved considerably since 1916, when Alexander Kerr wrote, "The only supply of pure water is rainwater collected and stored in underground cement reservoirs. We had to install student washbasins in a garage, and as for their baths—well, at least the Tyumie River is near the residence halls." In 1939, electricity was installed, but conditions were far from luxurious. An agricultural college had been established nearby so that the university could have access to milk and other products at cheap prices.

Nelson Mandela formed a friendship with another Xhosa student from the Transkei, Oliver Tambo, a year older than he. This was a friendship which grew deeper over the years, lasting through many changes and trials. Oliver Tambo was the son of a very poor farmer from Bizana, in the eastern Transkei. He attended the primary school at the Holy Cross mission in Flagstaff, a few miles from his native village. He was so brilliant in his studies that the missionaries sponsored him to study at St. Peter's school in Johannesburg, the most prestigious black boarding school of that day. The Transkei Bunga gave him a scholarship so he could attend Fort Hare University.

Unlike Nelson, Oliver was deeply religious, and remained so all his life. He wanted to become a pastor, and founded the Christian Students' Association at Fort Hare. On Sundays, they went to preach the Bible in neighboring villages. Nelson accompanied him on these evangelical trips, deeply impressed by his friend's brilliance, seriousness, and conviction. However, Oliver Tambo may have been influenced by Nelson Mandela as well, for he became a lawyer instead of a pastor. It was Mandela and Tambo who jointed to found South Africa's first black-owned law offices in 1953.

By sheer luck, Tambo escaped the raid on the Rivonia farm in 1964 because he was out of the country at the time. He became the expatriate President of the ANC. He spent most of his life in exile, and it was only in 1990, weakened by illness, that he was finally able to return to South Africa. He died three years later, at the age of seventy-six. This came almost exactly a year after the first free elections ever to take place in his country, elections of which he was one of the major architects. After his death, Nelson Mandela wrote: "I felt like the loneliest man in the world. Looking in his coffin, I felt that a part of me had died."

At least two of his professors at Fort Hare also made a lasting impression on Nelson. One of them was Z.K. Matthews, "the very model of an African intellectual," as he wrote later. The great novelist André Brink was also impressed by this man, and wrote:

> One day a black professor, Z.K. Matthews, a most wise and brilliant man, came and spoke to the students at our university. The hall was packed. He was enthusiastically welcomed, and some of us spoke of this event long afterward.

NELSON MANDELA

It was not so much for of his speech itself, remarkable though it was, as for the fact that this was the first time in our sheltered lives as whites, that we had met a black man who was neither a servant nor a laborer.[29]

Mandela notes that Dr. Matthews had been influenced by Booker T. Washington's autobiography, *Up From Slavery,* "which advocated success through diligent work and moderation." Professor Matthews was also an activist in the ANC. In 1936, he was a member of the delegation of eight people sent to Cape Town to protest the government's Natives Act (the law regulating indigenous suffrage), which abrogated black voting rights in the Cape Province. Nelson Mandela was one among many Fort Hare students who were deeply influenced by the teaching and example of this major figure.

Another professor who influenced him belonged to a family that had long been linked with Fort Hare. This was D.D.T. Jabavu, who had received a diploma in English literature from the University of London—an achievement which seemed at the time like "an impossible exploit," as Mandela said. Jabavu belonged to the Jele clan, whose ancestor Zwangendaba had fled the Zulu chieftain Chaka in the early nineteenth century. He was the first professor to teach at Fort Hare when it opened in 1916. He was so famous, and his name so linked to the university, that it was sometimes called "Jabavu's school."

Like university students everywhere, Nelson also engaged in extracurricular activities such as theater. He remembers fondly taking part in a production of a play written by another student in the troupe, based on the life of Abraham Lincoln. The author, Lincoln Mkentane, played the role of the great man he himself had been named after. He was also the only student taller than Mandela. The latter played the role of the assassin, John Wilkes Booth. Both cast

[29] André Brink, on a Bench at Luxembourg Garden.

and audience were filled with passion and enthusiasm for this drama of slavery, evil, heroism, and racial equality.

In spite of their school's relative isolation, lost in the southern African veldt, far from Cape Town and Johannesburg, these African students found many things in world history to kindle their imagination. They were quite aware of the status of their country as a world bastion of racial inequality and segregation. Such perceptions would have been virtually unthinkable for Rolihlahla when he lived at Mqekezweni (notwithstanding the disturbing speech by Chief Meligqili, a kind of anomaly). But at Fort Hare, the imbalance of the situation was obvious in daily life simply because he came in contact with many more whites than before. Alice was a white town and many white professors had children who attended Fort Hare.

Some Sundays, Nelson and a small group of friends would go out to a restaurant. But "eating out" for blacks at Alice was a very different thing than it was for whites. In those days, it was unthinkable for blacks to enter a restaurant by the front door, much less sit at a table. Instead, they had to go the kitchen entrance at the rear, where the kindness of the white Christian owners allowed them to purchase meals to go. They would then take their food and picnic under a tree somewhere.

At Fort Hare, they also learned ballroom dancing. Using an old phonograph, they would practice the waltz and fox-trot. Sometimes they would even slip into their best suits at night, sneak over the walls, and go the nearby village of Siwundla, to a black dance hall called *Ntselamanzi*. One night Mandela asked a pretty young woman for a dance, only to discover that she was the wife of one of his black professors! Shaking with fear, he accompanied her back to her table, and her husband. This memory can still give him a tremor over fifty years later.

But his main extracurricular activity was sports, especially long-distance running, soccer, and boxing. Perhaps as an outlet for his Thembu warrior-heritage, he continued to practice the latter for many years after moving to Johannesburg, even after his first marriage. In the 1950s, he was a member of the boxing and wrestling club in Orlando, a Johannesburg township.

In his memoirs, Mandela writes of the daily practice sessions with his son, Thembi, with whom he remained close after the divorce. He often took him to the boxing club. He described him as being "a bit on the skinny side, but an avid flyweight." The son greatly admired his father, who in his turn was touched and amused by his son's efforts to act like an adult. When he allowed Thembi to direct the training sessions, he was very strict with his father. He would even lecture him, saying "Mr. Mandela, you are wasting our time this evening. If you feel you can't keep up the pace, you should go home and stay with the ladies."

In 1969, his second son Makgatho came to Robben Island to inform him of his brother Thembi's death in an auto accident in the Transkei. It was a very heavy blow for the father. Thembi was only twenty-five, and had two small children of his own. "I have no words to describe the pain and loss which I felt. It left a void in my heart which nothing can ever fill." That evening his closest friend, Walter Sisulu, came to visit him in his cell. He said nothing, simply sitting with him and holding his hand in silence. "In a moment like that, there is nothing a man can say to another." The authorities refused him parole to attend his son's funeral.

In December 1940, Nelson Mandela received his B.A. degree in the subjects of English, History, Political Science, and Native Administration. His goal at that time was to become a civil servant or interpreter at the Bureau of Native Affairs. In those days, such a career was regarded as extraordinary, a top achievement for a South African black man.

Having a B.A. from Fort Hare University already made him part of an elite. During the first twenty years of its existence, from 1916 to 1935, the school had admitted a total of only 625 students. Of the 472 who had graduated up to that point, 111 had become pastors, 153 teachers or professors, sixty-eight civil servants and interpreters for the Native Affairs administration, and twenty-two agron-omists. Besides these, eight had become physicians and sixteen were studying medicine abroad. Only eleven were unemployed, and no information was available for the remaining eighty-three. These figures reveal a great deal about the role of Fort Hare University in black South African society.

Insults and Injuries

Nelson returned to Mqekezweni for vacation, and invited his friend Paul Mahabane to come along. He was the son of Zaccheus R. Mahabane, who had twice served as President of the African National Congress. His presence at the national conference of the ANC at Bloemfontein in 1930 was documented in the book *A Photographic History of the National African Congress.*[30]

One day the two friends walked to Umtata. In the streets of the town, Paul Mahabane refused to obey a white who accosted him. This man had never met Paul before, and had no idea who he was, but presumed to order him to run an errand. This was a common practice of the day. A white man could stop any black in the street, no matter what his age, and send him to buy cigarettes or stamps.

It so happened that this white man was a judge. Nelson knew this and was afraid. But his admiration for his friend's courage was greater than his fear. Right there and then, he made a major discovery: the established order of things could be challenged. A black man was not a lackey for whites. All you had to do was say No. This entailed risk, certainly—but when had blacks ever been able to live in this country without risk? As they walked away, the judge threatened Paul Mahabane, saying, "You'll pay dearly for this!" But nothing ever came of it. It was an empty threat.

---

[30] *Unity in Action: A Photographic History of the African National Congress, South Africa, 1912–1982,* The Congress, 1982.

"I began to realize that a black did not have to accept the constant, petty harassments and shame of everyday life," he wrote. Despite their arrogance, their self-assurance, and their threats, whites were not all-powerful. He now realized the truth of Rousseau's principle: no one is so strong as to always be the strongest in every situation. It was possible to refuse. What a discovery! When you have always accepted injustice because of fear and habit, and when the attitudes of your elders discourage any protest or challenge, then it takes only one experience of saying No to make this whole world start to crumble.

Nelson Mandela had been trained and conditioned from his earliest childhood to take the road he was now on. But given his nature, it was also only a matter of time before he would reach this sharp turn of awareness. It was as if destiny had decided his meeting with the son of the ANC activist, yet it was also no more than the means. From Mvezo to Qunu to Jongintaba's court at Mqekezweni, to the Bashee River, to high school and university beyond the Fish River: every one of these steps had brought him closer to this point. He could physically return across the Transkei border to the scenes of his youth as often as he wished. But he could never go back across this border within his new consciousness.

For some time now, his cultural mind had already ceased to be a unity like that of his ancestors and peers who had remained in the Transkei. Nor was he any longer capable of being assimilated into white culture, for that would mean accepting the assumptions of most of his young white peers, who never questioned the legitimacy of their own inherited privilege and power. Nelson Mandela's cultural mind was composed of layers, like geological strata left by the different experiences of his life. These can be grouped into four categories: African traditional aristocracy, white society, imprisonment, and liberation. As we have said before, this mixture, rare in South Africa or anywhere else, is the key to understanding his remarkable destiny.

It may well have been the memory of this incident in the streets of Umtata in 1940 which prompted Nelson Mandela to say at his trial in 1964, "Whenever they need something carried or cleaned, whites automatically look around for an African to do it, and it makes no difference whether or not that person is their servant."

The events of the late 1930s also began to affect life at Fort Hare, as they did the rest of the world. Since September 1939, the dean of Mandela's Wesley residence hall had established the practice of turning on an old radio every evening so that the students could follow the news on the BBC. The conflict on the other side of the planet was beginning to concern them in a number of ways.

First, a governing coalition had been formed in 1933, composed of the nationalist right and the liberal right. Hertzog, head of the nationalist party, was Prime Minister, and Smuts, head of the liberal party, was Second Minister. The two parties had been rivals, but were united against their common enemy, the British Party. At all costs, the Afrikaners had determined to keep the latter out of power. But in 1939, when the fundamental issue arose of what side South Africa would take in the war, the situation became dramatic.

Hertzog preached neutrality for two reasons: first, he and his party agreed with Nazi theories on racial superiority, and had always been in ideological sympathy with Hitler; and second, he hoped to take advantage of Great Britain's involvement in the war to have South Africa break away and declare independence—if necessary, even with military protection from Nazi Germany. This would be a stunning revenge for the humiliating defeat of the Boer War.

Jan Smuts, on the other hand, was resolutely opposed to the Third Reich, and wanted South Africa to support Britain and the Allies in the war against them. But the ministers were swayed by Hertzog in 1939, and voted seven to six in favor of neutrality. However, the Parliament reversed this decision and voted eighty to seventy-seven in favor of Smuts's position. The coalition had crumbled. Hertzog was forced to resign, and Smuts became Prime Minister.

During the previous year of 1938, when Nelson Mandela was still at Healdtown, Jan Smuts came to visit Fort Hare University.

This Boer War hero had later fought German troops in World War I in southwest Africa (now Namibia). He had previously served as Prime Minister from 1919 to 1924, so his visit to Fort Hare was a grand occasion and an honor for the university. Nelson and all his "black English" friends were deeply impressed, and thoroughly supported Mr. Smuts.

In 1939 and 1940, there were many animated discussions around the radio, after listening to the speeches of Churchill and the other events of the war. There were a few students who dared to argue that, when it came to the status of blacks, white men all belonged to the same party. One of them, named Nyathi Khongisa, went so far as to predict that British and Afrikaners would unite against the *swart gevaar* (the black peril). The other students whispered that he was a member of the notorious ANC, a radical black party whose reputation made most students afraid, including Nelson.

Under Jan Smuts's leadership, South Africa joined the Allies and declared war on the Axis. They sent a commando force to Libya, which included black and mixed soldiers, but they were allowed only to serve as unranked auxiliaries, and did not engage in combat or learn to use weapons. The white authorities knew better than to offer military training to blacks, who might someday use it against them at home. In any case, this expeditionary force never saw combat because they were taken prisoner by the enemy at Tobrouk in 1942.

After the coalition had broken down, Hertzog and D.T. Malan regrouped and founded a new, more extremist National Party in 1940. Eight years later, they would succeed in taking power, with Malan as Prime Minister and apartheid as their platform. But during the war years, the National Party worked to undermine the South African government's support of the Allies. This included both open opposition whenever possible, and covert action and terrorism—John Vorster himself, who would later become Prime Minister in the 1960s, was arrested in 1942 for a series of sabotage operations he led.

In 1939, the great majority of students at Fort Hare were staunch partisans of Smuts. They admired Great Britain in its heroic struggle, defending the values of its civilization against the Nazis. On this particular point, Nelson Mandela never wavered, nor gave in to cynicism. He reminded the judges at his trial in 1964, "I have always had the utmost respect for English political institutions, as well as for the judiciary system of that country. I consider the British Parliament to be the most democratic institution in the world. And the independence and fairness of its judiciary system continue to inspire my admiration."

Thus there were many reasons why the events of World War II had a far-reaching influence on the ideas of Nelson and his fellow students in their tiny university, isolated in the immensity of the southern African veldt. Yet in spite of his unwavering admiration for the British political system, his later experience in Johannesburg would bring him closer to the view of whites that Nyathi Khongisa had expressed during that heated discussion around the old radio at Wesley Hall.

He gradually came to believe that both British and Afrikaners had long conspired privately to set aside of their differences when it came to keeping blacks in the place. It was British capitalists who financed the mines where so many blacks had lost their lives that it was called "the world's most dangerous gold." The black housemaids and gardeners, who had been serving whites for centuries, were badly paid and poorly treated by Europeans all over Africa. Some were crueler and greedier than others, but even the "generosity" of the others began to appear to him as a form of humiliating paternalism. All white children in Africa attended school, no matter what their national origins or status. Yet there were never enough teachers or classrooms available for black children. The only reason he, Rolihlahla Madiba Dalibunga Mandela, had been able to go to school was because he belonged to a privileged minority—a minority whom the whites helped only because they counted on them to help maintain the status quo and keep the vast black majority in their misery.

In his sheltered university life, these issues only arose as topics of conversation. The arguments and positions that Nelson and his friends discussed remained on a purely theoretical level. Acting on them, one way or another, could be put off into a vague future. Nevertheless, most of them were aware that the day would come when they would have to take a stand. They knew that their privileged status as university-educated blacks entailed a great responsibility toward black South Africans as a whole. Nelson Mandela was especially aware of this responsibility because of his status as Thembu, and the expectations of his elders.

The events that took place at the University of Fort Hare in 1941 would lead him to make one of the most important decisions of his life. The vague future arrived sooner than expected, and his position could no longer remain on the theoretical level: he would have to choose between freedom and obedience.

General Strike at Fort Hare

Despite the strict discipline and structured life, in spite of the students' feelings of fear and respect for the administration, life at Fort Hare was not free of unrest. In his memoirs, published in 1968, Alexander Kerr, who had retired in 1948, wrote:

> In general, African students are more mature than their European counterparts, and show a greater sense of responsibility. Sometimes they express discontent, especially regarding the diet. Although food is plentiful, it is usually very simple, because of the low cost of tuition and board, which does not allow a great variety of food. And there are certain students who ask for privileges which cannot be accorded. This results in demands, and if no solution is found, these demands can lead to damage to property or persons, and a challenge to the proper operation of the institution.[31] Whatever the causes or consequences, there is no student who, at one moment or another, has not been witness to some sort of eruption of disorder.

In his own way, Alexander Kerr reveals the real material situation of the students when he speaks of the poor quality of their food. This is evidence of the extremely austere living conditions which prevailed at Fort Hare. Ntombizodwa, the sister of Dalindyebo, who was still living in Mqekezweni in the late 1980s, recalled clearly that

---

[31] An oblique reference to the student strike.

she was always hearing about the problems regarding the food at Fort Hare. Other sources of unrest are recounted in Kerr's memoirs, such as victims' complaints in 1921 about excessive hazing which led to the practice being banned on campus. But far more significant is his remark that students sometimes dared to challenge the content of the courses:

> Problems sometimes arose when students in a South African history class noticed a strange coincidence: it was always "Kafirs" who were responsible for starting all the wars, which were called "Kafir Wars." And when they studied the French Revolution, the most important chapter in the history curriculum, it sometimes happened that teachers and students found themselves on opposing sides.

All of this suggests that the students at Fort Hare were not at all docile and submissive lads. They were capable of mocking and opposing the administration, and of challenging the official version of South African history and taking opposing sides to their teachers regarding the French Revolution. Of course, this only shows that they had much in common with university students all over the world, criticizing the established order, criticizing the curriculum, and disagreeing among themselves as well. I would even go so far as to say that Alexander Kerr's memoirs reveal more about the students' behavior than those of Nelson Mandela himself. This is no doubt because he is speaking from the perspective of thirty years as head of the university. Mandela only speaks of his three years there, during much of which he was a timid and obedient student, still unsure of his political opinions.

There are conflicting versions about what actually happened in 1941, but it is sure that serious trouble broke out at Fort Hare in September of that year. In his supposed version of these events, Mandela explains that he had been elected to the student council, and supported two major student demands: better food and more power for the student council. After a number of vicissitudes,

Alexander Kerr gave Nelson Mandela an ultimatum: renounce his ideas, or be expelled. Kerr asked him to think about it during the two months' vacation, and to return in February 1942, but only if he were prepared to take part in the student council in the approved manner.

This version of events was written by the ANC in August 1961, when Mandela had just been arrested. For obvious political reasons, the author(s) of this article tried to glorify Mandela's role at Fort Hare, and his expulsion for having organized and directed the student strike.

The truth is that Nelson Mandela was never a member of the student council. His name does not figure in any minutes of their meetings. On September 10, 1941, the council members wrote a letter to the university's executive committee demanding the immediate dismissal of a boarding master who had struck a young black woman named Hilda in the kitchen. This boarding master, named Mr. Lundie, had long been detested by the students for his meanness and brutality, and this had created a tension that had been going on for months. When we add to this the other factors we have mentioned, such as the National Party's open support of Hitler, and the evolution of dissenting ideas in general among the students, we can understand why the atmosphere at Fort Hare was becoming explosive.

The student council met again on September 15, 1941. Yet the agenda for this meeting, dictated by the administration, contained nothing about the letter, or about the tense situation. Instead, there was to be a discussion of a party to be held in one of the halls. And the biggest problem to be resolved would appear to be that of how to transport chairs!

Outraged by the authorities' refusal to discuss the matter, the students decided to call an immediate strike, to last for three days. A group of Wesley residents, where Mandela lived, went to visit Beda, the Anglican residence hall where Oliver Tambo lived. Then they went to a third hall. Discussions were very heated between partisans and opponents of the strike, and some blows were exchanged.

Some students even talked to journalists, undoubtedly from the local press. But even this much publicity was extremely dangerous, for the university depended to a great extent on donations—from whites, of course.

It happened that Kerr himself was away in Scotland during this critical time. On Monday, September 18, Mr. Dent, Kerr's deputy, called an emergency meeting of the university board of directors. As might be expected, they came down firmly on the side of order and established authority. A boarding master is by definition irreproachable. Hilda's innocence was irrelevant. Besides, he had only slapped her, not punched her, as the students claimed. This last point seemed to be a decisive one as far as the board was concerned! And the fact the he was a white and she was a black.

In any case, they had decided that the truly guilty ones were the striking students. When the term ended, all of them (75 percent of the student body) were expelled. In order to be reinstated after the vacation, a student had to pay a fine, submit a letter of application, and another letter of apology for the strike. In his final report for that school year, Mr. Dent wrote:

> In September 1941, during the director's absence, the students demanded the resignation of the boarding master. They claimed this was because he had "brutalized" a native girl who worked in the kitchens. It was pointed out to them that there are proper channels for submission of such demands to the administrative council. However, they demanded that the deputy director take immediate action on this. If not, they threatened to "go on strike"—in other words, to stop attending classes. In spite of warnings from the faculty board, three out of four students carried out this threat for three days. The chairman of the university board met with the students, but refused to discuss their demands until they went back to classes. All except two of them returned to classes within the

time limit that had been given them. One of these two left the university to join the army. The other left the university, but asked to be readmitted. All the others who participated in the strike must pay a fine of one pound for disciplinary infraction, and write a letter of apology to the university board.

Who were these two students who refused to return to classes? This is very unclear. There was no occasion on which Nelson Mandela requested to be readmitted to the university, so he could not have been the second student. In 1988, Ntombizodwa recalled those days: "They [Nelson and Justice] had been sent home. Jongintaba had no idea what to do with them. He told them that they should write an apology, but they were stubborn. They said they would never go back there."[32] And it was certainly not Mandela who joined the army, though he did indeed wear a uniform for a brief period after leaving Fort Hare—but it was that of a night watchman at the gold mines in Johannesburg.

In spite of the confusion about these events, we can be reasonably sure of a few things. For the entire school term of 1941, Nelson Mandela was a student at Fort Hare, residing at Wesley Hall. He was not on the student council, and held no special position of responsibility in the strike, but he was certainly not on the sidelines either. One of his professors even remarked that he had a tendency to put himself in the limelight, but this could be interpreted as a hostile judgment by a conservative white elder of a young black man's natural brilliance, daring, and charisma, both in class and on the athletic field.

It is also certain that in September 1941, he joined with three-fourths of the student body in a strike in defense of a black female employee. Reliable witnesses reported that she had not just been

---

[32] Although Ntombizodwa speaks of both boys refusing to return, only Nelson had anything to do with the student strike. Justice was not a student at Fort Hare University, and had dropped out of high school in Healdtown.

slapped, but punched and kicked by a white boarding master (in fact, this man, Mr. Lundie, quietly resigned after this event in late 1941). Like the other strikers, Mandela was expelled. But unlike them, he alone never sent a letter of apology asking to be reinstated at Fort Hare. This is the most curious fact that emerges from this story. Its explanation is certainly not a simple one.

Flight

At Mqekezweni, Nelson was happy to be reunited with Justice, who was also visiting—he had quit high school and was living in Cape Town. But the Regent did not share in the boys' good mood. He was especially disappointed in his son, whom he hoped would finish high school and be admitted to Fort Hare. At first he took consolation in Nelson's greater seriousness, and urged him to write the letter of apology which would enable him to return to the university. Nelson adamantly refused.

A few weeks later, Jongintaba dropped a bombshell. He informed the two rebels that they were to be married. He claimed that he was very ill, with only a short time to live. Before joining his ancestors, he wanted his life to be in order, and this order included their lives as well. Everything had been arranged, the brides had been chosen, the families in agreement, and the *lobola* had already been paid. Stunned, there was nothing they could say.

In a biographical note written during his trial in 1964, Nelson Mandela recalled:

> My guardian felt that I should be married. He had great love for me, and watched over me with the same care that my father had shown. But he was not a democrat, and saw no need to consult me about who would be my wife. He chose a fat, well-bred young woman, paid the *lobola*, and arranged for the marriage. I fled to Johannesburg.

Missionaries have often used the European term "dowry" as a synonym for the *lobola*, but this is a distorted translation of the original custom. Because the *lobola* often amounts to a small fortune (a gift of from seven to fourteen head of cattle to the bride's family), missionaries have misinterpreted this custom, and even accused families of selling their daughters and buying their brides. The truth is that this ancient institution is a means of forming and solidifying alliances between families and clans. As John Henderson Soga pointed out, cattle are not just wealth, they are also living creatures which are powerful symbols for social and spiritual links between African families. To reduce the *lobola* to a mere financial transaction is to totally rob it of its meaning.

However, the 1930s brought drastic new economic conditions which did destroy the meaning of this custom. The huge number of young men who had left the countryside to work in the gold mines no longer had the means to engage in this form of transaction. Instead, they instituted the custom of paying money to the bride's family. This was indeed a kind of dowry, but it was the destruction of the *lobola*. This change was paralleled by the demise of polygamous marriages so that family structure and the institution of marriage among black South Africans came more and more to resemble those in the Western world. Nelson Mandela has been twice divorced and remarried, which is a pattern far more typical of European or American life that of his original tradition.

Despite these winds of change, in 1941, Jongintaba still took the *lobola*, together with the arranged marriage, as a sacred and solemn custom. He would not accept any discussion of his autocratic, patriarchal decision. In spite of his Ford V8 and his relations with white men, he was very much a local chief, deeply attached to tradition. The gulf that separated him from his two sons was immense, especially in Nelson's case, because of his advanced education. The prospect of an arranged marriage with women they had no part in choosing was like a regression to a world they had already left in their minds.

In his 1994 memoirs, Mandela says, "With all due respect to the young woman's family, I would have been dishonest to pretend that she was the bride of my dreams." In an effort to change the Regent's mind without a confrontation, Mandela went to his wife secretly and "confided" to her, pretending that he was already in love with another woman. But she was unable to influence her husband. "I felt that he was really leaving me no other choice," Mandela wrote. This was when the two young men decided to flee to Johannesburg. Looking at this with hindsight, one suspects they would eventually have left even if it hadn't been for the forced marriages. Justice had already been living in Cape Town. He was not as "serious" a young man as Nelson, and now that he had tasted life in the former capital city of South African, he had already decided that he didn't want to be "buried" in a "hole" like Mqekezweni. And, though Nelson had never been beyond Healdtown and Fort Hare, he had an even clearer sense than his brother of the vaster world beyond the Transkei and its customs. He had ambitions, though he could not yet say exactly what they were. His dreams were now of cities, buildings, electricity, and life in the streets, not of the cattle herds and prairies of his childhood. He wanted something else, and it was inevitable that he would leave sooner or later.

The brothers secretly prepared their escape. The most difficult problem was the watchfulness of the Regent, who was already suspicious of them. Finally, their chance came when he had to make a trip to Umtata for a meeting of the Bunga. Jongintaba left with a small suitcase, but terrified the boys by unexpectedly turning around and driving back to Mqekezweni. Seeing him coming, they were able to run and hide in a cornfield. When the road was clear, they stole two of his best cattle and sold them to a white man. They used the money to rent a car and drove to the train station. However, the stationmaster had been alerted, and refused to sell them tickets. They tried their luck at the next station on the line and succeeded.

The train took them as far as Queenstown, about sixty miles

north of Fort Hare. There they requested a permit to leave the Transkei, which was required for blacks. But the magistrate was suspicious, for he knew they were sons of a chief and sensed trouble. He telephoned to Umtata to speak to his superior, in whose office Jongintaba was sitting at that very moment. At first the boys were in panic, but Nelson rose to the occasion, bluffing his way as if he were already a lawyer. In fact, he did have some knowledge about the relevant laws from his studies at Fort Hare. He made full use of it now, informing the magistrate that he had no right to detain them. Reluctantly, he let them depart, but of course without the permit.

Now it was Justice who came to the rescue, through a friend of his who worked for a white lawyer. It turned out that this lawyer's mother was traveling by automobile to Johannesburg and would give them a ride. However, the kind lady demanded they pay her fifteen pounds. This was far more than the price of two train tickets, and was all the money they had left. But they had no choice and left in her car early the next morning. It was almost 500 miles to Johannesburg, a long drive in those days. Nelson and Justice were both seated in the rear, for it was unthinkable that a black would sit next to a white. Nelson sat quietly, in a somber mood. But Justice was restless and excitable during the whole trip, telling stories, imagining life in Johannesburg, even singing. His exuberance disturbed the old lady, for she was accustomed to blacks who were more quiet and respectful in the presence of whites.

It was 10:00 P.M. that same night when they finally arrived in the city. "Before us, we beheld a labyrinth of lights sparkling in the distance, so vast it seemed to stretch out in all directions," Mandela wrote. They had reached *eGoli*, the fabled City of Gold. Like all country people who see the lights of a very large city for the first time, they were dazzled. As they passed through the streets, Nelson squinted, for there were simply too many things to take in: huge buildings, billboard ads, and thousands of cars. But the main thing was the lights. "For me, electricity had always seemed like a novelty and a luxury," he wrote.

Nelson Mandela in traditional Xhosa costume in Johannesburg, in the early 1950s.

They had entered the city from the south, and made a large detour to the west, so as to reach the northern residential suburbs where the lady's daughter lived. Nelson and Justice were invited to spend the night in the servants' quarters of her home. They slept on the floor, but Nelson was so excited to finally be in Johannesburg that it seemed "like a feather bed" to him. He dreamed of his future there. However, as he wrote later, "This seemed like the fulfillment of a long voyage. But in reality, it was only the beginning of a much longer, and far more excruciating one."

I Have Crossed Famous Rivers

In 1942, when Nelson Mandela arrived in Johannesburg, the city was not even sixty years old. After George Harrison's discovery of gold ore in a desolate rocky spot lost in the veldt, a camp of gold miners quickly sprang up, which soon became a boom town and a city. In 1888, only two years after his discovery, there were already forty-six mines operating.

In 1887, there were 3,000 people there, mostly camped out. By 1900, it had become a city with a population of 166,000—an average of thirty people per day had been moving there. Perhaps the word "city" is a bit too elegant a term for this agglomeration, which had become the largest urban area in South Africa. Built around a downtown area with government buildings, police, banks, and stock exchange, a great deal of the new development took the form of suburbs: luxurious residential ones for whites, and slums for blacks, located conveniently near the active gold mines.

Although this was, and still is, one of the largest veins of gold ore in the world, extracting it was not an easy task. Most of it was in the form of dust mixed in sandy layers, and these lay deep, and ever deeper, as time went on. Today they are being worked at a depth of 6,000 to 9,000 feet underground. Until recently, it was only possible to extract a maximum of 95 percent of the gold dust. But new technology will enable the 5 percent left in the slag to be extracted in the future.

It was obvious from the beginning that these mines would require a very large labor force. And since profits were of supreme importance, the cost of this labor had to be as low as possible. This meant very harsh working conditions and a near-total disregard for security. And it meant most of the workers would be black.

A 1985 article entitled *The World's Most Murderous Gold*,[33] stated that "Every year, an average of 600 miners are killed. Since 1911, around 44,000 men have lost their lives in the gold mines of South Africa—only 3,000 of them were white." In 1985, 80 percent of the 460,000 black miners had no status as South African citizens. Most of them were from the pseudo-independent homelands. Both married and single workers lived in crowded "hostels," most of which were hellholes of misery and violence. Since members of the same tribe stayed together, ethnic rivalries and conflicts were constantly breaking out, which effectively prevented any sort of labor union from developing.

The gold-bearing region, called the Reef, forms a large arc in the Transvaal, part of which touches its border with the Orange Free State. Sparsely populated before the discovery of gold, it was also one of the poorest regions in natural resources. Virtually everything had to be imported from outside: building materials, water, and the most basic infrastructure for human habitation. Because of the lack of any sanitation system, a typhoid epidemic broke out in 1904, killing 2,000 people. Since then, it has been strictly forbidden to throw any waste water into the street. From the beginning, water was in such shortage that people often could not wash their clothes. Most miners were single (there were twenty-three men for one woman in 1910), and not in the mood to do laundry after a back-breaking day in the mines, even if water had been available for it. This led to the creation of a special laundry guild, composed of members of the Zulu Butelezi clan. The Zulu launders had to transport the dirty clothes to rivers far from Johannesburg

---

[33] Translation of "L'Or le plus meurtrier du monde," from an anthology entitled *Afrique du Sud* (Paris: Autrement, 1985).

in order to wash them. After the Boer War, they were forced out by big laundry companies.

However, for the white power elite, business was booming so fast the city's growth could scarcely keep up with it. In 1900, the stock-exchange building, built ten years previously, had already become much too small. While waiting for a new one to be constructed, a part of downtown Simmonds Street was chained off, and stock trading took place outdoors.

Housing has always been a major problem in Johannesburg, and in urban South Africa in general. From 1948 on, the apartheid law mandating strict racial separation of residential areas only aggravated this problem. It created a catastrophic housing situation which has still not been resolved today.

At the beginning of the twentieth century, there was already great poverty, and such a housing shortage that blacks and poor whites often lived in the same areas. This was far from agreeable to the latter, and when the Union of South Africa was created, a policy of more vigilance in racial segregation was instituted. For example, in 1911, a Johannesburg city councilman declared, "Today, there is a very large population of natives who are living permanently in the Union's cities. Some of them live in ghettos, but in Johannesburg they are scattered about in the poorest neighborhoods, living right next to whites." And a letter to the editor of the *Johannesburg Star*, a major newspaper, protested, "The natives should not be allowed to wear European clothes during working hours. Their employers should do something about this, because European dress gives them an exaggerated sense of their importance and equality."

In 1924, Johannesburg was declared as a white zone. This meant that blacks could only work, not reside there. Those who were not already living in peripheral ghettos were forced into townships outside the city. Between 1942 and 1946, the black population of the Johannesburg area doubled. The major area of this growth was the Southwestern Township, famously abbreviated as Soweto.

It was here, in this chaotically growing slum, that Nelson Mandela, like so many other black migrants, arrived in 1942. Nothing in his twenty-four years of life had prepared him for this experience. Since the end of the indigenous uprisings, the Transkei's geography (and its geology, since there was no gold there) had spared it most of the violence and misery of modern South African history. Nelson had in fact led a relatively sheltered life for a black. Village life had known little of the suffering that he would now witness, except for the growing depopulation of its young males, drawn by tragic illusion to exactly such circumstances as those in which he now found himself. As a Thembu, his traditional education and upbringing had been complemented by a white Christian upbringing, culminating in a university education. This made him a member of two African elites, and a rare bird indeed in this new setting.

His worldly experience was actually quite limited when he arrived in Johannesburg. His political gift was still latent, so that he had not yet even formulated any definite position. His studies and discussions at Fort Hare had taught him that the reality of South African history was far more complex and contradictory than the simple epics recounted by Joyi, the tribal elder. Although he remained proud of his Thembu heritage, he was already beginning to understand that there had to be a larger destiny beyond its scope, one in which all South African peoples were linked in their dealings with those of European origin.

The image of *eGoli* had not yet lost its luster, and the very lights of the city seemed to promise a future full of success and happiness. Also, the image of the miner had not yet ceased to symbolize strength, daring, and manhood, as in the fables told by Banabakhe Blayi to his rapt listeners beside the Bashee River.

This did not last long in the reality of Johannesburg. This fantasy world quickly crumbled before an onslaught of violence in every aspect of life: violence at work, violence in his living conditions, and the overall violence of a merciless exploitation of blacks, and the misery of their lives in general. Six months after Nelson's arrival, a black journalist wrote in the June 6 edition of *Bantu World:*

> I wonder if the authorities are really making any effort to deal with the gangs which roam the streets of Soweto day and night. Is it really impossible for them to rid us of these gangs of thugs, who victimize peaceful, law-abiding citizens of this city and this community? Personally, I think not. But as long as the authorities consider these almost daily assaults on members of Bantu society to be less important than infringements of the municipal code *[this refers to local segregation laws—Ed.]*, then I feel sorry for anyone who, like myself, is attempting to lead an honest life.

The day after their arrival, Nelson and Justice left the house where they had spent the night. They presented themselves at the offices of Crown Mines, the largest gold mine in Johannesburg, located in the southwest part of the city. Justice knew the *induna,* a kind of foreman responsible for hiring, whose name was Piliso. Normally, young men arriving from the countryside must present a letter from their chief to the *induna.* In those days tribal structures were still strong, and there were links between tribal authority and the urban industrial power structure. A few months earlier, Jongintaba had in fact written to Piliso to ask him to find a non-mining job—these were the most coveted positions—for his son. Since Piliso was only expecting one youth to arrive, Justice told him that Nelson was his brother, and that the Regent had sent a second letter for him, which had not yet arrived. Piliso not only came through with the jobs, but because of their status as sons of the Regent, he would not have them go to a hostel, and invited them to stay at his house.

So it was that Nelson found himself wearing a uniform, complete with boots and helmet. He was also furnished with a flashlight, a whistle, and a billy club. He was a night watchman, responsible for controlling any attempts to enter or leave the mines.

Everything seemed to be going splendidly for them. But, clever as the brothers were, they foolishly talked about their adventures to other members of the Xhosa community. News of their jobs at the mines reached Jongintaba at Mqekezweni. Beside himself with rage, he sent a telegram to Piliso. Nelson and Justice were fired on the spot. After only a few weeks, they were homeless and without work.

Nelson found lodging with one of his cousins, Garlick Mbekeni, who lived in the George Goch township. Impressed with Nelson's studies, he determined to find him a job more worthy of his talents than working at the mines. He decided to introduce him to a friend who worked at a downtown real estate agency, an educated man who seemed to know everyone. His name was Walter Sisulu. Walter listened carefully to Nelson's story of his life, his projects, and his reason for leaving Fort Hare. Mandela told him that his ambition now was to enroll at the University of South Africa and study to become a lawyer. Sisulu immediately thought of a liberal white lawyer he knew who might accept him as an apprentice.

This was a crucial meeting in Nelson Mandela's life for several reasons. One result was that he was later accepted as an apprentice at the offices of Witkin, Sidelsky, and Eidelman. This enabled him to go to law school, and eventually to become the first independent black attorney in the history of South Africa. A year after this, he would be joined by his old friend, and then associate attorney, Oliver Tambo, in opening South Africa's first black-owned law offices.

But on a deeper level, this was the beginning of a friendship and collaboration which would weather many years of joy and hardship. One of the Rivonia group arrested in 1963, Walter Sisulu would spend twenty years in the same prison with Mandela. Theirs is a friendship which is still strong today.

Another momentous consequence of this meeting was getting to know the Sisulu family, and the new world and exciting ideas of black political activism. Walter himself had been a member of the ANC for about two years.

Naturally, these developments took place over time, rooted in the everyday experience of life as a black man in Johannesburg in the 1940s. His own political awareness was growing fast, spurred by the everyday petty humiliations from whites, and nurtured by his discussions with Walter and other fellow activists, including a white communist, who also worked as an apprentice at the law offices. Gradually, he came to realize that political struggle was not an option, but a necessity.

> I am unable to determine the exact moment when I became politicized, the moment when I knew that I would devote my life to the struggle for freedom. I had no epiphany, no singular revelation, no moment of truth, but a steady accumulation of a thousand slights, a thousand indignities, and a thousand unremembered moments produced in me an anger, a rebelliousness, a desire to fight the system that imprisoned my people. There was no particular day on which I said, Henceforth I will devote myself to the liberation of my people; instead, I simply found myself doing so, and could not do otherwise.

Nevertheless, there were decisive encounters which fired his imagination and awareness. One of these took place some eighteen months after his arrival in Johannesburg, at a time when his ears were wide open to a new political language. One evening in 1943, at Walter Sisulu's home in the Orlando ghetto, he met Anton Lembede. This lawyer, of very modest family origins, expounded the most radical black nationalist ideas he had yet heard. According to him, the destiny of black people was to liberate all of southern Africa from foreign occupation, and to awaken a collective African consciousness. Whites in South Africa were unable to see things except through the lens of race, so Africans had no choice but to also look at them in this way. Lembede's ideas struck a resonant chord in young Nelson's mind.

A year later, a militant group had formed around Lembede.

Its members included Sisulu, Tambo, Mda, Nkomo, Mandela, and others. It was the beginning of the ANC Youth League. This organization developed rapidly into a veritable Trojan horse, which later took control of the old ANC. Indeed, 1943 was a decisive year for the future of South Africa.

In December 1942, Jongintaba died at Mqekezweni. Nelson had received the news too late, and arrived there the day after the funeral. He spent a week in this village of his childhood. It seems fitting to end this story of the early life of Nelson Rolihlahla Madiba Mandela with his own reflections as he left Mqekezweni:

> There is nothing like returning to a place that remains unchanged to find the ways in which you yourself have altered. [...] In Xhosa, we say *Ndivelimilambo enamagama*— "I have crossed famous rivers." It was this proverb that was in my thoughts on the way back to Johannesburg. Since 1934, I had crossed all the famous rivers of my country: the Bashee and the Kei on the way to Healdtown; and the Orange and the Vaal on the way to Johannesburg. But I had many rivers yet to cross.

Map

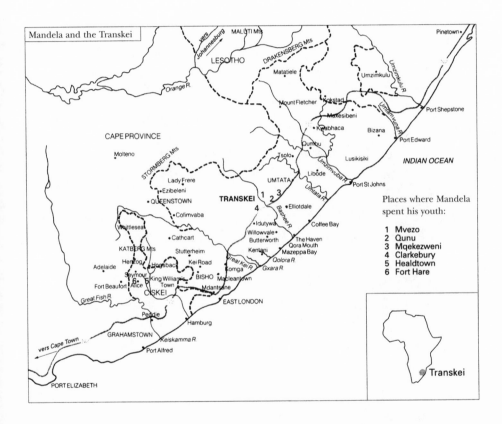

Mandela and the Transkei

Pinetown

vers Johannesburg

MALUTI Mts

LESOTHO

DRAKENSBERG Mts

Matatiele

Umzimkulu

Umzimkulu R.

Orange R.

Mount Fletcher

Kokstad

Maxesibeni

Umtamvuna R.

Port Shepstone

CAPE PROVINCE

Kwabhaca

Bizana

Port Edward

Molteno

Qumbu

Lusikisiki

INDIAN OCEAN

STORMBERG Mts

Tsolo

Umzimvubu R.

Libode

Lady Frere

UMTATA

Port St Johns

Ezibeleni

TRANSKEI

1

2 3

Places where Mandela
spent his youth:

QUEENSTOWN

4

Umtata R.

Bashee R.

Elliotdale

Cofimvaba

Idutywa

Coffee Bay

1 Mvezo

Whittlesea

Willowvale

The Haven

2 Qunu

Cathcart

Butterworth

Qora Mouth

Mazeppa Bay

3 Mqekezweni

KATBERG Mts

Kentani

4 Clarkebury

Stutterheim

Great Kei R.

Qolora R.

5 Healdtown

Adelaide

Hertzog

Hogsback

Kei Road

Komga

Gxara R.

6 Fort Hare

Seymour

King William's

BISHO

Macleantown

Fort Beaufort

Alice

Town

Mdantsane

6

CISKEI

Mdantsane

Great Fish R.

EAST LONDON

Peddie

Hamburg

vers Cape Town

GRAHAMSTOWN

Keiskamma R.

Port Alfred

Transkei

PORT ELIZABETH

Chronology

May 31, 1902
The Treaty of Vereeniging, ending the Boer War.

May 31, 1910
Founding of the Union of South Africa.

January, 1912
Founding of the South African Native National Congress, which later changed its name to the African National Congress, or ANC.

1912
Birth of Walter Sisulu in Engcobo, Transkei.

1917
Birth of Oliver Tambo in Bizana, Transkei.

July 18, 1918
Birth of Rolihlahla Madiba Mandela at Mvezo, Transkei.

1920
Mandela's mother moves to Qunu.

1927
Death of Henry Gadla, father of Nelson Rolihlahla Mandela. Rolihlahla leaves Qunu to live at Mqekezweni.

January, 1934
Mandela undergoes traditional initiation ritual marking the end of childhood. He enters the missionary boarding school at Clarkesbury.

March 18, 1936
Birth of Frederik De Klerk in Johannesburg.

1937
Mandela enrolls at Healdtown, a black prep school.

February, 1939
Mandela enrolls at Fort Hare University for blacks; meets Oliver Tambo.

Late 1942–early 1942
Mandela leaves the university, then flees Mqekezweni for Johannesburg.

1942
Nelson Mandela works at several jobs in Johannesburg, from night watchman at a gold mine to a white collar job in real estate. He begins law studies and meets Walter Sisulu.

1943
Mandela moves to Orlando township and works as a legal apprentice for a liberal white lawyer.

April, 1944
Founding of the Youth League of the ANC, headed by Anton Lembede. Nelson Mandela married to Evelyne Ntoko Mase.

1946
Mandela moves to 8115 Orlando West.

1947
M. P. Mda becomes president of the ANC Youth League, with Tambo as vice-president, and Mandela as secretary.

May 28, 1948
The National Party wins the (white only) elections. Daniel Malan becomes Prime Minister.

December, 1949
The ANC holds its national convention at Bloemfontein. The Youth League gains control of the leadership.

February, 1950
The first apartheid laws go into effect: the Population Registration Act, and the Immorality Act.

May 1, 1950
The ANC organizes a strike. Nineteen people are killed by the police.

June 26, 1950
National day of protest.

June 26, 1952
Campaign of disobedience to unjust laws begins. Mandela's first arrest.

1953
Nelson Mandela becomes head of the Transvaal ANC. With his old friend Oliver Tambo, he opens South Africa's first black-owned law offices.

June 25, 1955
The People's Congress of South African Peoples meets at Klipton.

1956
Nelson and Evelyne Mandela are divorced.

December, 1956
Nelson Mandela arrested. The trial for high treason begins (156 people charged).

June 14, 1956
Nelson Mandela married to Momzamo Zaniewe Winifred (Winnie) Madikizela. The ANC splits, and the Pan-African Congress is created.

March 21, 1963
Massacre at Sharpeville: 69 dead, 180 wounded.

March 29, 1961
The trial for high treason ends in acquittal for all.

April, 1961
Mandela goes underground.

May 31, 1961
Declaration of the Republic of South Africa.

December 16, 1961
Bombs of sabotage explode at Durban, Johannesburg, and Port Elizabeth.

January 11, 1962
Nelson Mandela leaves South Africa, traveling in Africa and in Europe.

July, 1962
Mandela returns to South Africa.

August 5, 1962
Nelson Mandela arrested.

November 7, 1962
Mandela sentenced to five years in prison.

July 11, 1963
Leaders of the MK (Umkhonto we Sizwe, or "Spear of the Nation") are all arrested at Rivonia.

October 9, 1963–June 12, 1964
The famous Rivonia trial at Pretoria. Mandela and his colleagues are sentenced to life imprisonment, narrowly escaping execution. They are sent to Robben Island penitentiary.

June 16, 1976
Massacre at Soweto. At least 618 dead and 1,500 wounded. Over 13,000 arrested and sentenced to prison terms.

May 16, 1977
Winnie Mandela banished to Brandfort.

April 1, 1982
The Rivonia group are transferred to Pollsmoor prison, near Cape Town.

August, 1988
Nelson Mandela is transferred to Victor Vester prison, in Paarl.

September, 1989
Frederik De Klerk becomes President of South Africa.

October, 1989
The Rivonia group released from prison.

February, 1990
Nelson Mandela freed.

May 4, 1990
The Groot Schuut Accords.

June 30, 1990
Abolition of apartheid.

August 6, 1990
The ANC renounces the use of arms.

February 4, 1991
Winnie Mandela goes on trial.

November, 1991
Nelson and Winnie Mandela officially separated.

December 20, 1991
First meeting of the CODESA (Convention for a Democratic South Africa).

March 17, 1992
Referendum on reforms.

April 16, 1992
Nelson and Winnie Mandela divorced.

May 15, 1992
CODESA II

June 17, 1992
Massacre at Boipatong.

September 7, 1992
Massacre at Bisho, Ciskei.

April 1, 1993
CODESA III

April 10, 1993
Chris Hani murdered.

April 24, 1993
Death of Oliver Tambo.

September 7, 1993
Creation of the Transition Executive Council (TEC).

October 15, 1993
Nelson Mandela and Frederik De Klerk are awarded the Nobel Peace Prize.

November 18, 1993
Adoption of the new constitution.

April 27, 1994
The first free and fair elections in the history of South Africa. Nelson Mandela elected President.

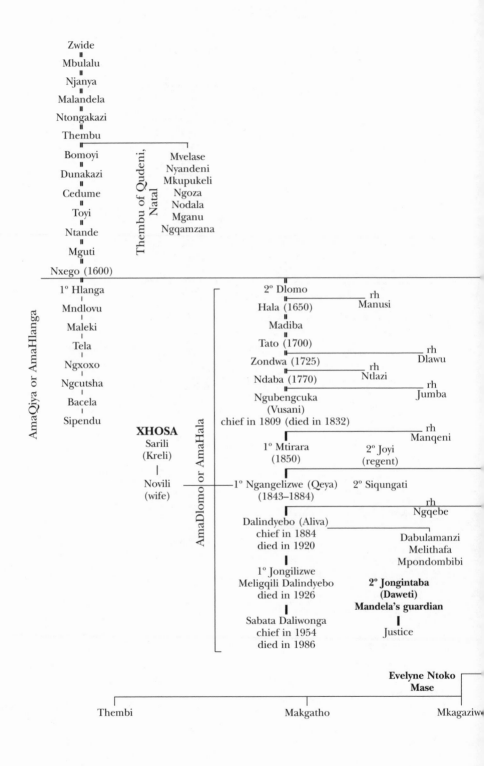

Royal Thembu Genealogical Chart

l: ruling branch

rh: right-hand house

sh: secondary house

Ishiba: secondary house.
 This branch is not permitted
 to rule. See pages 25–26.

Sarili was the Xhosa chief during
the cattle killing. His daughter,
Novili, married the Thembu Chief
Ngangelizwe.

first-born son
Ndungwana

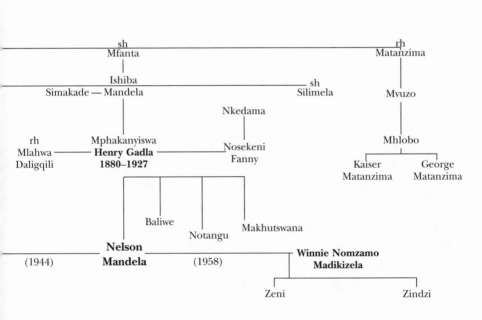

A note on the literature of apartheid:

The South African political, economic, and cultural situation during apartheid inspired many writers of dissent, both black and white. This produced a literature of extraordinary quality and passion, which offers one of the best introductions to post-apartheid South Africa. Among the most important recent authors are: Nadine Gordimer, J.M. Coetzee, Breyten Breytenbach, André Brink, Njabulo Ndebele, Mike Nicol, Karel Schoeman, Denis Hirson, Esk'ia Mphahlele, and Sipho Sepamila.

Bibliography

Breytenbach, Breyten, *The True Confessions of an Albino Terrorist* (New York: Farrar, Strauss, Giroux, 1984).

Brink, André, *On the Contrary* (New York: Little, Brown & Co., 1994).

Brink, André, *A Chain of Voices* (New York: Viking Penguin, 1989).

Brink, André, *The Ambassador* (New York: Summit, 1986).

Kerr, Alexander, *Fort Hare, 1915–1948: The Evolution of an African College* (Pietermaritzburg: Shuterand Shooter, 1968).

Mandela, Nelson, and Fidel Castro, *How Far We Slaves Have Come! South Africa and Cuba in Today's World* (New York: Pathfinder Books, 1992).

Mandela, Nelson, and Desmond Tutu, *The Rainbow People of God* (New York: Image, 1996).

Mandela, Nelson, *Long Walk to Freedom* (New York: Little, Brown & Co., 1995).

Mandela, Nelson, *Mandela: An Illustrated Autobiography* (New York: Little, Brown & Co., 1996).

Matshoba, Mtutuzeli, *Call Me Not a Man* (Johannesburg: Ravan Press, 1979).

Soga, John Henderson, *The Ama-Xhosa: Life and Customs* (Johannesburg: Alice Lovedale Press, 1931).

Wilson, Monica, and Leonard Thompson, *A History of South Africa* (Cape Town-Johannesburg: David Philip Publishers, 1982).

About the Author

Born in the Eure-et-Loir province west of Paris, Jean Guiloineau is an academic consultant for the literature curriculum of the University of Paris. He now resides in Arles, in southern France, where he works as a writer and translator.

He is the author of many books, including a complete biography of Nelson Mandela. He has also translated Mandela's autobiography into French, as well as works by Toni Morrison, Henry Miller, Leonard Cohen, Virginia Woolf, and André Brink.

Also available from North Atlantic Books

Tenzin Gyatso:
The Early Life of the Dalai Lama
By Claude B. Levenson
Translated by Joseph Rowe
$14.95 trade paper, 168 pp.
ISBN: 1-55643-383-2

Tenzin Gyatso focuses on the formative years of the fourteenth Dalai Lama, before he became a worldwide presence and peace activist. It is the authoritative biography of the first twenty-four years of his life as told by a close personal friend and prolific journalist, Claude B. Levenson. This biography follows the long and arduous path that the Dalai Lama traveled from his birth in 1935 to his exile to India at the age of twenty-four.